Paragraph

A Journal of Modern Critical Theory

Volume Volume 44, Number 1, March 2021

Sarah Kofman and the Relief of Philosophy

Edited by Jacob Bates-Firth and John McKeane

Contents

MIX
Paper from responsible sources
FSC™ C013985
FSC www.fsc.org

Introduction

JACOB BATES-FIRTH AND
JOHN MCKEANE

The Relief of Philosophy

This collection of essays sets out to read the work of Sarah Kofman in all its vitality. This means contributing to the study of the work itself, as well as setting it in its intellectual context. But it also means measuring the philosophical ambition that was Kofman's, which allows her to speak to questions of our own age in an untimely way. For instance, much has recently been made of the possibility of writing and thought helping us to deal with a hostile world (hostile politically, economically, generationally, environmentally). Should we follow Boethius in turning to the consolation of philosophy, for instance, a greater connection with the ideal world distracting us from the ugliness of the material one?

This is certainly one resonance of our title *the relief of philosophy*, and to some extent it speaks to the way Kofman was always concerned to read philosophy and psychoanalysis together. However, fantasies of purity or the ideal are at some distance from her thinking. To this extent, *the relief of philosophy* can also mean *relieving* philosophy of its idealizing tendencies, its tradition, its self. Whether as a dedicated reader of Nietzsche or as a member of deconstructive circles alongside Derrida, Lacoue-Labarthe and Nancy, Kofman did not shy away from combative engagements, insisting that imposed binaries be rejected as 'metaphysical', and that matters instead be seen as a continuum or sliding scale, however uncomfortable that might be.

Although psychoanalysis is a constant interlocutor, and life-writing and autobiography form intense presences in her written work, she does also remain dedicated to philosophical rigour, to its counter-cultural untimeliness. Here we might see a third sense of *the relief of philosophy*: relief in the sense of standing out or standing apart.[1]

Paragraph 44.1 (2021): 1–10
DOI: 10.3366/para.2021.0350

www.euppublishing.com/para

Reading her work, it is impossible to escape the impression of a thinker revelling in the rejection of partially thought-through arguments. For instance, her reading of stoicism via Nietzsche would make short work of many of that school of thought's recent returns. Does the call to rediscover the rhythms of nature, as a way of distancing oneself from the hostile modern world, not package that nature in an ultimately comforting or reassuring way, and misleadingly so, given the measureless, unjust violence of the natural world? Things unfold similarly with Epicureanism, that supposed art of living, which (again via Nietzsche) Kofman denounces as representing just another withdrawal from the world, just another narrative of salvation.[2]

Over and against such schools of thinking, Kofman argues for a tragic sensibility. She writes that philosophy must be read critically, without acceptance of its claims to special status:

> the most tyrannical will to power there is, [philosophy] imposes its own Apollonian measures on the Dionysian measurelessness of nature; in its will to be the first cause, to be God, it creates a reassuring world, one created in its *image*, a sort of double, a colossus to protect it against the violence of becoming, against suffering and death. In this sense, all philosophy is *tragic*. (NS, 167, emphases original)[3]

This seems to suggest the removal of various protective layers (elsewhere, Kofman speaks of different philosophies as compressive bandages, as having soporific qualities, even as being akin to opium). To do so is not to increase the amount of suffering in question, but merely to approach it in a different way — no longer as an adjunct, but as the very stuff of life. Whilst she sees philosophy as ultimately always leading back to tragedy, this does not mean that philosophy has always — or ever — been at ease with this tragic destination. Indeed, this unease leads it to take the presumably opposite form of comedy: in Kofman's words, '[philosophy] hides this [tragic destiny] by playing a *comedy*: the comedy of morality'.[4] Because this is a shying away from truth, from (unbearable) nature, Kofman finds such comedy absurd. Whilst one senses that there is a pleasure in making such denunciations, then there is also a rigour for Kofman, who pursues the double approach of becoming utterly conversant in the philosophical tradition whilst refusing to accept certain of its most important axioms. But if that tradition, in Cartesian France especially, is often defined by its method, what form does Kofman's method take?

Kofman's Worldly Method

We have begun to see Kofman rejecting many of the major senses in which philosophy acts as *relief*, even as she engages in productive ways with the polysemy of that term. But what do such refusals to transcend or sublate the world mean for the way in which she understands that world, its materiality, its presence, and our presence within it? Remembering Raphael's *School of Athens*, does rejecting Plato's upwards-pointing finger mean one must endorse Aristotle's downwards-facing palm?

A striking aspect of Kofman's critical method can be of use here. On numerous occasions she takes an approach that flickers between being experimental in the high deconstructive style, and scholarly in the traditional one. This can be seen in *Socrate(s)* (1989), *Explosion I* (1992), *Explosion II* (1993), and notably in the essay translated in this volume, 'And Yet It Quakes! (Nietzsche and Voltaire)' (1994). It consists of a detailed and extensive engagement with the texts being read, often letters, to the point where the distinction between Kofman's own writing and that of her objects of study starts to break down. In the text we have translated, for instance, it was not possible to apply the standard convention of breaking off longer quotations into blocks separated from the main text: this would have left little continuous main text to deal with, especially in the first and fourth sections, where roughly two-thirds of the paragraphs end in substantial quotations.

In other words, here is a thorough engagement with the materiality or literality of texts, with the world as something given, already there, to be engaged with in immanence rather than transcended through critical appropriation. In fact, this approach is suggested in her early work too: in *Nietzsche et la scène philosophique* (1979), for instance, there are multiple moments where Kofman's and Nietzsche's voices merge, partly in line with the tradition of scholarly ventriloquization of one's object of study, but also far beyond that (we find her discussing a particular viewpoint as 'the first conviction that must be present in your mind if you need, feeble and suffering men, consolation' (NS, 213)).[5] This means that rather than cohabiting peacefully, the strands of ventriloquizing one's object and adopting a critical position external to him or her pull apart from one another. This is to be aligned with her adoption of perspectivism, born less from approval of, than simply from long familiarity with, irreducibly multiple perspectives (see her two mother figures as presented in *Rue Ordener, Rue Labat*, or her two father figures in Nietzsche and Freud, the multiplicity problematizing any single authoritative narrative whilst also making the latter's absence more keenly felt).

The main object Kofman ventriloquizes is Nietzsche — the thinker whose work tells us that if there is to be a fusion or alignment with the sheer superficiality or mendaciousness, it should come not from weary compromise but from vital will. Whether in the *amor fati*, the Eternal Return, or Dionysus as the god of bodily pleasure, Nietzsche always leads us back towards the world and its force. In this sense it is fitting for Kofman's essay to cite Galileo's *eppur si muove*: she aligns herself with this insistence on movement and energy, pointing out through ventriloquizations of Voltaire and Nietzsche that the earthquakes at Lisbon and Ischia allow us to conceive *both* the force of transcendental metaphysics that must be overcome ('"moral evil" provok[ing] greater disasters than natural catastrophes do'), *and* the force of this transvaluation or overcoming.[6]

In short, then, Kofman's material, often literalizing approach to text sits alongside her reading and ventriloquization of a thinking of ever-closer union with the world in all its vital becoming or novelty. This is not to be read simply in terms of the thereness of the static, real, existing world, but with a view to the way this world is replenished in its ever-shifting, ever-superficial appearance.

Salvation Fictions

'Now, what Nietzsche shows', Kofman states, 'is that philosophy, since Socrates (...) has possessed the same *will* as tragedy: healing the wounded gaze in mastering the contradictions of becoming through the invention of those salvation fictions which Being, Substance, Thing-in-itself, etc. are.'[7] On this view, the history of philosophy, if it can be seen as a philosophy that departs from any and every ontological concept, becomes the history of a fiction, and what is more, a fiction concerned with salvation. We shall unpack the precise way in which Kofman makes such conceptual moves shortly. But first, we should ask whether it is Nietzsche alone who shows her this. And is this, in its incontestable simplicity, really what Nietzsche shows her? No!

As regards the first question, in an early text, above even Freud (on whom Kofman published six books), Melanie Klein is lauded:

> In order to comprehend the history of metaphysics, Kleinian categories seem more suitable than those of Freud. There is an impossibility of metaphysics accepting

mixture in order to conserve intact the good object: its desire for purity, for integrity and for originary innocence come back to the fear of losing the good object, through contamination or through fragmentation.[8]

What is the value of Klein for Kofman's project of distancing herself from any and every 'logocentric enclosure' (PU, 76)? It is the value of a psychoanalysis which 'touches on the originary constitution of objectivity (...) without allowing a formal theoretical ontology to be thus derived' (PU, 77), an ontology which is anathema to Kofman. In this text, on her colleague Jacques Derrida, Kofman proposes the philosophical horizon of 'a *psychoanalytic graphology* (...) grafted more onto [the work of] M. Klein than onto Freud' (PU, 77, emphasis original). Yet Klein is rarely cited subsequently, and nearly two decades later is castigated, in passing, on the basis of being 'derivative of Freud and his concepts [and] derivative of the categories and oppositions of metaphysics'.[9] Is this to say that little to no trace of this horizon is to be found?

No! Kofman's texts, through to her last and including some of her most 'intimate', are visibly replete with the aspects of Klein which were relevant to her cause. Rousseau, for example, in the account Kofman gives of his thought in a later text, is readily identifiable with the 'impossibility of metaphysics' detailed a decade earlier, in the text above: in a general fashion, he strives 'to deny all ambivalence, to separate radically the good and the bad breast'.[10] '[A]ll of Rousseau's work (...) can be envisaged as a manner of making reparation to the body of the mother', as an expression of a need 'to keep intact and pure (or rather [...] to construct) and to interiorise a good image of the Mother, idealised and divinised' (RF, 125). And this need, in Kofman's account, leads to the elaboration of a series of metaphysical conceptions of sexual difference and sexual identity, particular to Rousseau but associable with 'all philosophy past and to come' (RF, 75): men and women are allocated discrete, transcendent models, and their resemblance condemned. The final ambition of the enterprise: the creation and the protection of a transcendent mother, a transcendent good object, the ontologically arbitrary infinitization of a fantasy for the sake of emotional relief.

Kofman, operationalizing Kleinian concepts against the history of philosophy (and in the name of her Nietzsche), asserts that Rousseau meets up here with the principal metaphysical desire: a desire for pure and permanent presence, which she implicitly refers back to the good object: 'This entire description of perversion is very Platonic: [for

Rousseau] the more each sex distances itself from the model which ought to be its own, the more it distances itself from Truth, the more it is unrecognisable, the more it loses its ontological consistency and identity' (RF, 111). Trickily, which perhaps explains the general lack of care to cite or refer readers to Klein, this operationalization is undertaken not with the intent of founding or verifying psychoanalytic truth but of putting any and all truth to rest. Kofman, who does not dread a loss of faith in ontological or personal consistency ('I don't know who I am, perhaps I am nothing', she states an interview in *Le Monde*) and who was hostile to every metaphysics and every culture which depends on such a faith, is affirmative rather of Nietzsche's definition of '[the] "ego" much more in terms of surpassing and displacement than substance'.[11]

In a still later analysis of a *pseudo-mémoire* written by Diderot, *The Nun*, Kofman provides a further elaboration of this thesis:

> at this moment, where institutions (. . .) were crumbling from the ground up, will the price to pay not have been the maintaining, at least at the level of fantasy, of the illusion of a certain permanence, that of an unshakeable feminine nature? And the appeal to [this] nature in Diderot, as in Rousseau, will it not have contributed simply to the restatement as concerns women of the very religious prejudices which these Enlightenment *philosophes* strove at the same time to destroy?[12]

The restatement of theological prejudices 'as concerns women' represents, for Kofman, the conservative preservation of an entire system of beliefs, a preservation which emerges less from a love of truth than from a dread of madness ('[my] involvement with "women" [. . .] stems from my interest in the problems surrounding madness'[13]). It is on this basis, the rejection of a surreptitious theism, that Kofman is critical of the discourse of the *philosophes*, rather than out of the immediate desire for an equality or a moral justice built in their image.[14] Such is, for Kofman, the fatally conservative and misogynistic flaw of a definitional feminism which would seek to determine and valorize specifically 'feminine' characteristics. That of Luce Irigaray, for instance: 'With her, we are back to Rousseau!' (CS, 43).

A Mendacious 'Philosophy'?

This is the truth as concerns sexual difference and sexual identity in philosophy, a corrective 'last word'. Really? In 'diagnosing' the installation by the *philosophes* of an eternal feminine in this manner, does Kofman claim to dissolve illusions and to substitute for an aberrant perspective an objective truth? In the same vein, in identifying 'being' as a mendacious 'salvation fiction' and in lambasting the need of Rousseau, among others, for 'ontological consistency', does Kofman take the absence of such consistency as a *sine qua non* and thus make a determinate ontological statement ('being is becoming') at the very moment she conceives of a break with ontology?

No! Or rather, we cannot say. In moving beyond any 'logocentric enclosure', Kofman wilfully relinquishes the relation of her statements to a self-identical truth which would enable such statements to be taken at their word. Claiming across several late-career interviews to be a philosopher 'on condition that [this term] is set in quotation marks' (SS, 111), Kofman disbars herself from the metaphysical tradition while retaining a rigorously — or pseudo-rigorously — integrated perspective on it.[15] Kofman states that, for her part, the title of philosopher is kept on the grounds of a commitment to 'rigorous conceptual thinking' (SS, 111) and her possession 'fundamentally (. . .) (of) a will to truth, even if this to say that truth does not exist' (EE, 22). The nature of her philosophical practice, now predicated fundamentally on this non-relation to truth, is characterized in the following terms:

> Taking up great texts (. . .) I always come to stating, starting with certain details, some *original things*; this gives my readers an *impression of truth* (. . .). Starting with certain details, the reading of great authors is totally *renewed*. I would define myself such as (. . .) a reader who nonetheless *displaces* quite considerably the texts read. (EE, 24, emphases added)

We are told it is a discourse whose outcome is no longer intended to be the enunciation of 'truth' but the production of the new, one sign of which is an 'impression of truth' in a reader, an impression which has no metaphysical value and which is an indication simply of the reader's *sentiment* of having experienced novelty. Such coordinates are repeated elsewhere in similar terms: 'it is the end of philosophy, one cannot constitute a system any longer. I would define myself essentially as a reader, a *productive* reader since I completely *renew* the reading of great texts, but *I no longer believe in a truth*.'[16]

Tellingly, in an earlier text on the history of aesthetics, Kofman states that 'with art, there plays out not a simple work of the negative, but a work of mourning un-sublatable by any mastering dialectic' and that 'beauty (. . .) is as though in mourning for philosophy', an infinitized 'mourning' which is also a broadside against the good object(s) classically furnished by ontological concepts.[17] What Kofman offers the metaphysical tradition is the sight of itself relieved of everything it traditionally ought to accomplish through its requalification as an artistic discourse: not as a distanced aesthetics, which would be to retain a relation to metaphysical purity which every letter of her work militates against for the sake of radical change, but as a transformative embodiment and evocation of this 'beauty' itself. Philosophy is openly handled as a possible artwork the entire value of which may perhaps be understood not in relation to truth but in relation to a principle of creative innovation, an evaluative criterion which, following Nietzsche, she sometimes names 'life' and which she frames as an explicitly anti-ontological criterion.[18]

In the end, what Kofman seems to learn from Nietzsche (and Klein) may, to certain ears, be taken not as an education in the ontological primacy of becoming and the needful dissimulation of this primacy over the course of the history of metaphysics, but in the artistic or 'vital' possibilities that can emerge from laying claim to at once a non-belief in truth and a 'philosophical' right to affecting and effective ontological statements, albeit dislocated from truth. She teaches us that a 'dialogue between deaf ears' can be just that and that we can do other things with the 'awful spectre of relativism' evoked by the apparent loss of the object than simply repudiate it or refuse to repudiate it (NO, 54).

The consequences of Kofman's thinking on these questions are, along with the readings of Kofman which we are very proud to make available through this volume, emphatically, left for a reader to determine.

NOTES

1 The term also chimes with *la relève*, a common French translation of the Hegelian term *Aufhebung*. Although this concept involves a certain amount of negativity — an abolition, suppression, or abrogation — it also has a positive counterpart, an extolling, a lifting or heaving up (*re-lever* in French). Something that is *aufgehoben* is annulled in its current existence, but lifted up into some other realm, plugged into a dialectical system. This can be pictured if we remember that the term is used in everyday German for making vegetable pickles or preserves, which is to say things stored for later. See 'Aufheben' in Barbara Cassin (ed.), *Dictionary of Untranslatables: A Philosophical Lexicon* (2004; Oxford: Princeton University Press, 2014), 71–6. Unless otherwise indicated, all translations are our own.

2 Sarah Kofman, 'La comédie du stoïcisme' and 'Figures du sauveur' in *Nietzsche et la scène philosophique* (Paris: Galilée, 1986), 143–61 and 163–93, hereafter NS.
3 See also Sarah Kofman, 'La Naissance de la tragédie' in *Explosion II: les enfants de Nietzsche* (Paris: Galilée, 1993), 77–132.
4 See NS, 167.
5 See also Alan D. Schrift: 'I find myself uncomfortable with remarks from *Nietzsche et la métaphore* like this one: "aphoristic writing and metaphorical style distinguish men from one another and keep at a distance the common run, the 'democratic' plebs, those who are not clean"', from '*Le mépris des anti-sémites*: Kofman's Nietzsche and Nietzsche's Jews' in *Sarah Kofman's Corpus*, edited by Tina Chanter and Pleshette DeArmitte (Albany, NY: State University of New York Press, 2008), 75–90 (81).
6 See Sarah Kofman, 'And Yet It Quakes! (Nietzsche and Voltaire)' in the present volume. Here she is quoting and ventriloquizing Voltaire.
7 Sarah Kofman, 'L'espace de la césure' [1978] in *Mélancolie de l'art* (Paris: Galilée, 1985), 73–86 (75, emphasis original).
8 Sarah Kofman, 'Un philosophe "unheimlich"' [1973] in *Lectures de Derrida* (Paris: Galilée, 1984), 11–114 (102–3), hereafter PU.
9 Sarah Kofman, 'Interview with Sarah Kofman' in *Shifting Scenes*, edited by Alice A. Jardine and Ann M. Menke (New York: Columbia University Press, 1991), 104–12 (109), hereafter SS.
10 Sarah Kofman, *Le Respect des femmes* (Paris: Galilée, 1982), 125, hereafter RF.
11 Sarah Kofman, 'Apprendre aux hommes à tenir parole' [interview with Roland Jaccard], *Le Monde* (27–28 April 1986), vii; Sarah Kofman, 'Le/les "concepts" de culture dans les *Intempestives* ou *La double dissimulation*' [1973] in NS, 289–318 (315). For what we may interpret, though not without caution, as an account of the libidinal stakes of such a definition, see Christopher Bollas, 'The Transformational Object' in *The Shadow of the Object* (New York: Columbia University Press, 1987), 13–29.
12 Sarah Kofman, 'Séductions' in *Séductions* (Paris: Galilée, 1990), 37–8.
13 Sarah Kofman, 'Entretien avec Christa Stevens', *Stoicheia* 4:2 (1987), 37–51 (38), hereafter CS.
14 On this point, see the distinction established between Voltaire and Nietzsche at the conclusion of the essay of Kofman's collected in the present volume.
15 Sarah Kofman, 'Subvertir le philosophique ou Pour un supplément de jouissance' [interview with Evelyne Ender], *Compar(a)ison* 1 (1993), 9–26 (11), hereafter EE.
16 Sarah Kofman, 'Relire Simone de Beauvoir, entretien avec Catherine Rodgers', *Les Temps modernes* 601 (1998), 16–37 (34, emphases added). The structure of Kofman's thought is presented by her friend and colleague Jacques Derrida as 'a sort of open quasi system, a coherent network that is

nonetheless without closure, at once consistent and structurally interminable, an incomplete-incompletable seriality'. Jacques Derrida, 'Introduction' in Sarah Kofman, *Selected Writings*, edited by Thomas Albrecht, with Georgia Albert and Elizabeth Rottenberg (Stanford, CA: Stanford University Press, 2007), 1–34 (18).

17 Sarah Kofman, 'The Melancholy of Art', translated by Jennifer Bajorek, in *Selected Writings*, 205–17 (210).

18 Sarah Kofman, 'Nietzsche and the Obscurity of Heraclitus', translated by Françoise Lionnet-McCumber, *Diacritics* 3, 39–55 (51), hereafter NO. In Kofman's essay in the present volume, following Nietzsche, this principle seems to appear under the name of 'Dionysus', and also that of Nietzsche '"himself"', in all his de-substantiating 'substance'. In a metapsychological framework, we may perhaps qualify this as an affirmation of the hold of the death drives over an ego which instinctively repudiates them and strives to forget them, which amounts to an attempt on Kofman's part to transform what the 'ego' can be.

Kofman's Affirmative Creation: Moral Law, Dom Juan and the Limits of Maternal Debt

CILLIAN Ó FATHAIGH

> For me, the philosophical interest of this text on Dom Juan is to pose the question of the law. Once we refuse an unjust patriarchal law, unjust towards women in particular, can we for all that do without all law, that is do without all debt? Can we deny all debt? Is this 'debt' only a Judeo-Christian inheritance or does life itself imply this duty? One, for example, of affirming life in creating?[1]
>
> Sarah Kofman, *The Question of Women*

Introduction

Sarah Kofman is generally not considered a thinker of justice. And yet, as this epigraph makes plain, the question of how to 'create' a more just law is clearly an important concern for her. Significantly, this problematic is explicitly presented as an issue of moving away from unjust conceptions of societal debt and patriarchal law. Moreover, as this epigraph also makes plain, this problematic is particularly prominent in her 1991 text on Molière's *Dom Juan* (1682).[2] This is surprising, both because the text has received sparse attention (even relative to the general neglect of Kofman's oeuvre), but also because of its title: 'L'art de ne pas payer ses dettes' (The art of not paying one's debts). On the title alone, we might assume that the text concerns avoiding obligation and law. As we will see, it is precisely the failure of such an 'art' that places the question of law in such sharp relief.

Paragraph 44.1 (2021): 11–25
DOI: 10.3366/para.2021.0351

www.euppublishing.com/para

In this article, I will argue for the importance of Kofman's text on *Dom Juan*. This is a significant text not only because it places the questions of law and authority in a prominent position, but also because it can help highlight the importance of these questions across Kofman's corpus. To develop this, I turn to Kofman's reading of Kant and Freud, showing how both they and Dom Juan are presented as operating in the same sexual economy. Building on this, I connect Kofman's position on Nietzsche's perspectivism to her reading of *Dom Juan*. I argue that Dom Juan's failure to reject all debt is tied directly to his dependence on gender binarism, and particularly an essentialized view of the maternal. Overall, I argue that in these texts, and most notably in 'L'art de ne pas payer ses dettes', there is an effort to develop an idea which I label 'affirmative creation'. This remains a suggestive and provisional idea for Kofman, where the form that such creation would take remains unclear. However, what is clear is that this creation must move beyond traditional gender categories and particularly the paternal and maternal.

Dom Juan's Double Failures

At the title suggests, 'L'art de ne pas payer ses dettes' is from the outset interested in questions of law and payment. Indeed, in the preface, both Kofman and Jean-Yves Masson state quite clearly that they wish to interrogate 'the relationship to paternal law and the question of unpayable debt' (AP, 9). Though Dom Juan might at first appear an odd candidate for such considerations, it is because Dom Juan rejects the paternal law so systematically that he can provide a resource for thinking through the possibility of rejecting all debt: it is exactly because Dom Juan uses and abuses promises that he is 'more, or something else, than a seducer' (AP, 70). For Kofman, Dom Juan's acts of seduction are simply a means to an end:

> seduction, for Dom Juan, is only one of the *means*, perhaps the most important, of exhibiting his fundamental intolerance to keeping his word (. . .). His refusal (. . .) of internal or external obstacles follows from his 'fundamental project': refusing to pay his debts. (AP, 70)

The standard depiction of Dom Juan, shared by Kierkegaard, is that he is a single-minded seducer.[3] For Kofman, however, this is only a symptom of Dom Juan's overall aim: the rejection of all debt. Rather than offering a justification for moral law, then, Dom Juan seeks to establish himself as the ultimate authority, bound to no one.

Yet Dom Juan has much greater aims than simply rejecting all obligation on this earth; he wants to reject all debt beyond it too. In challenging the conception of Dom Juan as just a seducer, we come to see that his target is not women at all, but rather God *himself*: 'beyond women, then, it is always God whom he provokes and it is with him alone that he debates; in the end, it is God to whom he refuses to be committed or indebted' (AP, 96). His insistence on breaking all contracts is, therefore, a 'contract of "radical atheism"' (AP, 76). In this way, we come to see the Nietzschean dimension of Dom Juan. He challenges the 'common representation that creates a God, a Supreme Creditor, under the model of the most primitive of social relations that ties a debtor to his creditor' (AP, 76). Dom Juan thus rails against a 'mercantile' (AP, 77) and miserly God who would add up the negative and positives of our actions. Dom Juan challenges God by continuously swearing to the heavens, while systematically breaking his oaths. This echoes Dom Juan's father who prayed to the heavens that he be given a son.[4] For Kofman, God granted this prayer and so Dom Juan's atheism is an effort to resist being inscribed within a line of supposedly miraculous births in the Judeo-Christian tradition, such as Isaac or Samuel, whose lives are devoted in advance to God. Dom Juan does not simply reject the idea of God giving life in general, but also the idea that God might have given him his own life. This is 'a vital defence: he can only affirm himself by denying/(de)negating (*(dé)niant*) the existence of God, or only by wishing he was the son of no one — *causa sui*' (AP, 114). Dom Juan's rejection of debt, therefore, is a total rejection of his own paternity: both his own father and God who made his miraculous birth possible. His refusal of debt is not simply a dismissal of social bonds, but a challenge to God the father.

In this context, then, God takes the only reasonable action for a divine, paternalistic being who finds himself in such a position: he kills Dom Juan. At first, this might appear a problem for Kofman's reading. The traditional interpretation of Dom Juan's death is that it is a simple *deus ex machina* aimed at reinforcing a conservative social and religious framework. Ultimately, Dom Juan is punished. Though Kofman acknowledges this, she also brings out how this ending has far greater consequences than may at first appear. For even after Dom Juan's death, his own debts live on, 'proving that there is something that does not run entirely smoothly in the system of debt' (AP, 116). These outstanding debts — be they to his many fiancées or Sganarelle's unpaid wages — are never repaid. Dom Juan demonstrates the hypocrisy of a society which would allow him to acquire such debts through nobility alone, but also the hypocrisy of a God who cares little for the debts that are incurred in this world. Finally, what Dom Juan's death exposes is that there is no ultimate source of authority that can coerce him into keeping his obligations.

Having elaborated how Dom Juan rejects debt and obligation to society and God, Kofman goes one step further, demonstrating that, in spite of this, Dom Juan does not succeed in rejecting *all* debt. It is not in his success at rejecting debt that Dom Juan becomes interesting, but rather in his failure. Her reading shows that in quarrelling with God *the father*, he leaves the door open for God *the mother*. Kofman stresses that if Dom Juan rejects a God who conceives of justice as a balance sheet of wrongs and rights, he does so only by substituting an essentialized maternal God of unconditional love and grace, who would exercise total forgiveness without consequence (AP, 120). To challenge the paternal law, Dom Juan effectively installs another form of authority: the maternal. Dom Juan is able to 'kill' his father only because he is '"supported" by the maternal help of Nature' (AP, 120). Hence, the radical atheism that Dom Juan espouses is undermined by the fact that Dom Juan 'makes way for a "religious" sentiment for Nature' (AP, 120). It is this maternal representation of Nature, as she who offers unconditional love, that ultimately limits Dom Juan's resistance to paternal law. When we turn to the sexual economies of Kant and Freud, we will see the greater implications for this and for our understanding of Dom Juan's failure to reject all debt.

This failure has an important consequence for Dom Juan's desire for self-creation. As we have seen, his challenge against God *the father* is to be his genesis, his '*causa sui*' (AP, 114).[5] Kofman defines Dom Juan as this creative desire: 'Dom Juan is the desire for continuous re/creation, which is a correlate of his refusal to pay his debts to his father and to God' (AP, 119). He understands each new act of seduction as an opportunity to 'to self-create, to recreate himself' (AP, 119). Yet the positing of an alternative God, one that would be maternal and natural, limits the scope of this creation. Not only does Dom Juan not assume responsibility for his own creation, delegating it instead to a higher authority, but this also takes place within a gendered binary. As Kofman points out, 'This is why Dom Juan, in spite of his desire for self-creation, is not entirely a modern Nietzschean hero *avant la lettre*' (AP, 120). Dom Juan may slay this paternal God, but in doing so he strikes a bargain which still limits his individual capacity for creation and self-determination. In the final section, I will demonstrate that this is important not simply for *Dom Juan*, but exactly because Kofman ties creativity to the potential of a new and more just moral law, one tied to 'affirming life in creating'.

Kant and Freud's Sexual Economy

To begin accounting for Dom Juan's failure, we must turn to an unlikely ally: Kant. Indeed, given that Dom Juan lies and seduces his way across most of Italy, stopping only occasionally to defraud someone of money, we might not necessarily imagine a relationship to the chaste Prussian. However, it is precisely around the authority of paternal law where these figures intersect. Kant often plays an important though subtle role in Kofman's work. Kofman's most thorough engagement with Kant occurs in 1982 with the publication of 'The Economy of Respect: Kant and Respect for Women', where she brings forth the misogyny inherent in Kant's account of moral law.[6] Thirteen years later, we see this argument return verbatim but this time in relation to Freud and his explanations of the origins of law: through this, Kofman demonstrates a shared sexual economy across Freud, Kant and Dom Juan, one based on the maternal as natural and a source of unconditional love.

From the outset of her Kant essay, Kofman makes it clear that the relationship between women and the categorical imperative is at issue: 'To respect women: is this simply to obey the categorical imperative which requires respect with regard to the other as moral personage?' (ER, 187). Kofman outlines two notions of respect at work in Kant: one which concerns the respect for superiors, such as the respect of a child for their parents (comparative respect); and the second, the respect that each of us deserves due to our equal dignity as human beings (moral respect). However, women have a curious and disruptive position within this framework, which ultimately collapses the distinction between the two (ER, 187–8). If this distinction breaks down in relation to women, it is ultimately because women are understood as a means to educate men in morality. They must exist prior to respect, in order for respect to emerge. The relationship between men and women is seen as a 'model, a prefiguration of moral respect' (ER, 188). This is true in two ways. The first refers to sexual relationships between men and women, whereby feminine 'modesty', in its denial of the sexual, is what leads men away from sensuality and towards decency and thereafter morality (ER, 192–3). The second is the more literal sense of education, whereby women, as mothers, are responsible for educating children: 'moral respect certainly "begins" with respect for women, for mothers, a necessary "preliminary" for teaching "terminal" moral respect' (ER, 200). Women, therefore, stand outside Kant's chronology of moral respect: they deserve respect as human individuals but must at the same time exist prior to respect.

However, for mothers to stand outside this chronology comes at a cost for Kant. He insists that for there to be an *a priori* ground for moral law, we must first have an idea of the law, which can then be personified and mediated (ER, 199). Anything else is 'pathological' and risks 'seducing' men towards sensibility, where they confuse the determination of law in general with the moral law, which is itself unfigurable (ER, 199). However, through the role of women as means and medium to communicate respect, this system is disrupted. The preliminary position of women here means that there is no way to know the moral law outside of its being first mediated through them. It is precisely because women personify moral law, as 'mothers' or 'religious myths', that they present such a problem and risk seducing men once again (ER, 200). Thus, 'chronologically, the "personification" always comes first, before the knowledge of a priori moral principles, and this risks the contamination of all subsequent "representations" of the moral law' (ER, 200).

Kant's effort to ground a moral law in *a priori* principles is disrupted by these bothersome women. As Natalie Alexander has shown, with these women 'the purity and authority of Kant's moral law breaks down: reason is always infused with the sensual figuration, the *a priori* with the *a posteriori*, universal respect with the desire of domination, the masculine with the feminine'.[7] Kofman demonstrates how Kant's account needs to appeal to the mediation of this law and that women represent such mediation; in so doing, the *a priori* and *a posteriori* merge into one another.

Kofman's position on Kant here is interesting not simply because of the argument itself, but also in its repetition thirteen years later. In 'Un autre Moïse, ou la Force de la loi' (Another Moses, or the Force of the Law), we see the return of a similar analysis of Kant that featured in the 1982 text.[8] Indeed, aside from the exclusion of the second and third sections, the discussion of Kant is nearly verbatim. As we will see, framing her discussion of Freud in terms of moral law in Kant is decisive, particularly in exposing a similar sexual economy in Freud's account of the origin of the law.

Kofman analyses Freud's interpretation of the statue of Michelangelo's Moses in the church of San Pietro in Vincoli (Saint Peter in Chains). She demonstrates how Freud views Moses not as an enforcer of the law, angrily lashing out at those worshipping the golden calf, but instead as a representation of the superego itself. Against previous interpretations, Freud interprets Moses as supressing his rage and internalizing it, so as to protect the ten commandments that are in his right hand. From this, we are led by Kofman through the various accounts that Freud offers of the origin of the law (AM, 58). To resolve this, Freud makes a move that we can now recognize as Kantian: he relies on women as a 'means' to address this problem. For Freud on Kofman's account, women play 'the fundamental role (. . .) in the education of men in morality' (AM, 66). This 'educational role' includes the way that women discipline men's language, 'constraining men to use more and more refined jokes (*mots d'esprit*)' (AM, 66). These refined words are a way of 'indirectly discharging their aggressive and sexual tendencies' (AM, 66). Here, then, within the economic account of the law, women educate men on how to externally express their violent desires. Similarly, in *Civilisation and Its Discontents* (1930), we see the mother embodied in the figure of the goddess Anangkè, 'teaching men the necessity to bend themselves to the law of time and of death and to defer the satisfaction of their desires' (AM, 66). It is worth noting the remarkable overlap that Kofman's text highlights between Kant and Freud: it is not simply that the woman presents a problem for their account, but it is in education, understood as a phased process overseen by a female tutelary figure, that this problem emerges.

We see, thus, that Freud and Kant operate in a similar sexual economy. It is not simply that they rely on similarly misogynistic language, but that both their systems struggle with the mediation of moral law, and the way it conflicts with their desire for an *a priori* foundation. This struggle takes place around women and the almost identical educational role that both insist on attributing to women in general, but particularly to motherly figures.

However, there is a further point tied to this sexual economy that Kofman makes particularly explicit in terms of Freud.[9] Kofman ties this rejection of the mediation of moral law to a specific conception of love and the maternal. Throughout the Moses essay, the term *ad oculos*, 'obvious on sight', is repeated at several points (AM, 56, 59, 66, 73). We see this, for instance, in the maternal Anangkè, who announces '*ad oculos* the necessity to renounce *carpe diem*' (AM, 66). This is how the suppression and delay of desire is communicated. Rather than interpreting or speculating, Freud maintains that he is simply discovering a truth that was there all along. This refusal to acknowledge his interpretations as interpretations stems, Kofman suggests, from this desire for an objective foundation, but it is also a denial of the mediation of the maternal that he had previously insisted upon (AM, 73). And this point leads us to another text on Freud published four years earlier, *'It is only the first step that costs'*, where it is also a question of the *ad oculos* exhibition of the moral law.[10] Here, though, this need for the objective is tied directly to a view of the maternal as natural and of Mother Nature: 'As if he was afraid that the mother, Nature, might not have loved him enough to reveal her secrets to him, without it costing him' (PC, 77). Freud is concerned that the maternal will not offer an unconditional gift, 'free love', but instead that it will come at some form of expense (PC, 74). This desire for an unmediated relation to moral law is thus tied closely to the sexual economy at work in Freud's text. When we come to Nietzsche's perspectivism, we will see that the limitations of the natural and maternal represent fundamental targets for the affirmative creation that Kofman advocates.

It is this sexual economy which returns us to Dom Juan. What Kofman brings forth is that in both Freud and Kant the desire for this *a priori* ground relies on a form of misogyny: women are not worthy of respect in themselves, but only as a means which causes this respect to emerge. Importantly, though, this is not only a question of the use of sexist tropes, but also a way of idealizing and essentializing the maternal. It is here that Dom Juan's maternal God joins this sexual economy. We see that this essentialism does not simply apply to Freud's justification of moral law, but also to Dom Juan's resistance to it. What Dom Juan and Freud share is this link between the maternal and the desire for a gift of unconditional love. As we have seen, Dom Juan presents this as crucial in his battle against the paternal creditor–debtor perspective of God. He hopes to replace such a deity with a Mother Nature who would love with no conditions attached, and thus 'dedicates a genuine religion' to Nature, who he believes will offer him 'this gift of life without recompense, a gift of free love' (AP, 119, 115). It is Dom Juan's reliance, therefore, on the maternal as a ground of resistance against paternal law which leads him into the same sexual economy as Kant and Freud.

Beyond Maternal Creation

Dom Juan's resistance to the paternal debt relies on a misogynistic sexual economy, one which Kofman also brings forwards in Kant and

Freud. However, in spite of these similarities, there is a significant difference: Dom Juan's desire for (self-)creation. After all, though Kant and Freud wish to explain the authority of the current (patriarchal) law, Dom Juan seeks to move beyond that. This is exactly why, in our epigraph, Kofman asks, 'once we refuse an unjust patriarchal law, unjust towards women in particular, can we for all that do without all law, that is do without all debt? (QF, 70). Yet, alongside Kofman's implicit scepticism about the possibility of rejecting all debt, there is also a positive condition given: 'One, for example, of affirming life in creating?' (QF, 70). This is what I have labelled 'affirmative creation'. Kofman does not, in this instance, specify the medium of this creation: is it artistic creation, intellectual creation or some other form?[11] However, what the text on Dom Juan does point to is one of the targets of this creation: binary categories, and it seems particularly gender binarism. It is this which conjoins 'L'art de ne pas payer ses dettes' with Kofman's reading of Nietzsche.

For Dom Juan is blind not only to his mother — who remains absent in the text — but also to the authority of the maternal. To bring this out, Kofman introduces a discussion of the Oedipus complex towards the end of the essay. In one of the few articles to give this text any sustained attention, Brian O'Keeffe is critical of such a move, suggesting that this 'psychoanalytic grid' limits Kofman's reading, halting the 'impulse' of her essay and repeating 'the only plot [that] psychoanalysis knows'.[12] Yet, O'Keeffe's criticisms here miss what I consider to be the fundamental point of the essay: Dom Juan does not reject *all* debt, because he remains indebted to the maternal. Kofman underlines how Dom Juan seeks to possess the mother and be seduced by her in each of his 'conquests', and how he seeks to liberate both the mother and himself from the paternal law: 'And through all these women, is it not her, and Dom Juan himself by identification with her, that he seeks to free from the masculine, patriarchal and divine?' (AP, 119). Though Dom Juan wishes to 'free' the mother and seeks from her an unconditional love, this does not remove her from a position of authority. The mother can still speak in terms of the law, and it is for this reason that it is to her alone that Dom Juan is obligated: 'The mother (...) is the only one to which, in a displaced and sublimated way, he recognises his debt' (AP, 119). Rather than overthrowing a higher authority, Dom Juan finds himself swapping one obligation for another, the paternal for the maternal. This debt limits the scope of Dom Juan's self-creation, in spite of the fact that this is his defining characteristic: he is 'this desire for continuous re/creation' (AP, 119).

Dom Juan falls short on his own terms. Importantly, positioning the mother as a God figure is not simply the result of Dom Juan's desire to challenge the paternal, but it also reflects the authoritative position and potential that the mother can assume.

Indeed, this question of self-creation in *Dom Juan* brings us to the Nietzschean dimensions of the text. Throughout this essay *Dom Juan* is placed in constant dialogue with Nietzsche. Kofman makes this very explicit in the footnotes, citing *The Genealogy of Morals* six times, often using long block quotations. However, despite the apparent similarities, it is exactly their different relations to the maternal that separate Dom Juan and Nietzsche. Dom Juan relies on an essentialized maternal that he is indebted to, whereas Kofman brings forwards a Nietzsche whose perspectivism challenges any such essentialism. For Kofman, as we will see, this perspectivism is a precondition for the affirmative creation she proposes.

Throughout her work, in diverse ways, Kofman develops an argument around the importance of creation in Nietzsche. She proposes a form of universal perspectivism in Nietzsche, whereby no perspective can have access to unmediated truth. A distinction is then drawn between the artistic mode of viewing the world, which acknowledges this perspectivism, and the ascetic which insists on a moral and truth-focused view of the world: 'The camera obscura of painters is immanent in the eye of each viewer and does not give a pre-existing reality. Rather, it constitutes for each his or her own "reality" which is in fact one with "appearance".'[13] Indeed, the theological idea of being created in God's image can 'seduce only those who [are] incapable of being the poets and/or sculptors of their existence'.[14] The idea of unveiling nature is 'the perspective of those who are unaware that, behind the veil, there is yet another veil', who are not strong enough 'to love appearance for appearance's sake'.[15] This perspectivism, therefore, is the exact opposite of the type of essentialism and naturalism that we saw at work in Freud and Dom Juan. On Nietzsche's terms, Dom Juan's 'art' of rejecting debt is no art at all.

It is in the figure of Dionysus that this perspectivism becomes strongly tied both to creation and affirmation. Dionysus is the representation of this affirmation of life as appearance. He is 'the symbol *par excellence* of the affirmative force; the symbol of the unlimited and unrestricted amen to life' (EX, 88). Dionysus is creative insofar as he both destroys previous values, and creates new ones *in the name of life*: 'It is this which the symbol of Dionysus means above all:

the pleasure of the negative is in necessary correlation with the pleasure of creation in affirming new tables of values' (EX, 350). Dionysus represents perspectivism because he establishes new values and removes the previous categories that were taken to be given and natural.

Perhaps Kofman's best-known reading of Dionysus occurs in her essay on Baubô. There, Kofman rehabilitates this marginal figure in Nietzsche's work. Baubô is a goddess, understood as a 'female double of Dionysus' (B, 45), and responsible for Dionysus' own rebirth in reminding his mother of her own reproductive powers. There is much to say about this reading, but what is important here is that Baubô does not exist as a rival or replacement for Dionysus; rather, the thrust of Kofman's reading is to make explicit the 'feminine' aspects of Dionysus that Nietzsche's misogyny has allegedly repressed (B, 27). In emphasizing the 'feminine' aspects of Dionysus, through Baubô, Kofman shows us that not only does Dionysus affirm life, he also affirms it beyond the distinction of masculine/feminine: 'Dionysus, a Greek god anterior to the system of theological oppositions, crosses himself out (*se rature*) of the distinction between the veiled and unveiled, masculine and feminine, fetishism and castration' (B, 46). The disruption of these oppositions is thus fundamental to Dionysus' affirmation of life and his creative nature.

We see, therefore, that for Kofman creation and affirmation take place only through the disruption and overcoming of categories, and this includes the maternal and paternal. The attention that Kofman devotes to the maternal here offers further support to the arguments of Tina Chanter and Kelly Oliver, both of whom have recognized the important position of maternal authority in Kofman's work.[16] However, this also allows us to highlight a difference between the account of maternal authority we see here and that of Kelly Oliver. Oliver proposes that Kofman has an ambivalent relationship to maternal authority: 'The riddle or enigma of Kofman's writing is why the trajectory of her work seems to lead both toward and away from the mother' (E, 182). Yet, our account above would suggest that, rather than being enigmatic, the maternal simply limits the form of creation that Kofman wants to valorize. Indeed, Oliver acknowledges that, for Kofman, 'by having it both ways, Nietzsche/Dionysus can give birth to himself without killing off the mother; rather, he gives birth to himself through his identification with fertility' (E, 179). But, as Oliver herself also acknowledges, it is exactly on this 'having it both ways' where she and Kofman disagree. For Kofman this is an essential part of overcoming the 'theological' oppositions, whereas for

Oliver this is the very logic of fetishism.[17] As such, rather than leading to a 'fascination with the ambivalent maternal' (E, 186), Kofman's insistence on Dionysus defying such categories means that the maternal can only be seen as restrictive. As we have seen, this desire for self-creation is not only part of Kofman's reading of Nietzsche, but also forms a fundamental part of her interpretation of Dom Juan.

Yet Dom Juan is no Dionysus. Though like Dionysus he seeks his own continuous self-creation, he cannot embrace the universal perspectivism that Dionysus and Baubô represent. Dom Juan instead relies on an essentialized version of the maternal, to whom he remains indebted. In so doing, Dom Juan reinscribes the oppositions of masculine/feminine or paternal/maternal that Dionysus resists. For Kofman, Dom Juan's act of creation re-enforces the authority of these categories at the exact moment he should be seeking to move beyond them. It is for this reason that in our epigraph, Kofman posits an alternative to Dom Juan: affirming life through creation. In the figures of Baubô and Dionysus, we see that it is the ability to free oneself from these categories that is central to the creative and affirmative process. And this is why Kofman returns to Oedipus at the end of her reading of *Dom Juan*. Though the father may be gone, the maternal is in the ascendant and this reinscribes *parental* authority and debt, at the exact moment when Dom Juan wishes to detach himself completely. Though the terms may have changed, the contract remains.

Two important consequences follow from this reading. The first is that, far from an isolated text, Kofman's 'L'art de ne pas payer ses dettes' is in close dialogue with many of the central questions of her work. Indeed, it is particularly useful in highlighting her substantial interest in the force and authority of law. The second consequence is a distinctly political interpretation of Nietzschean perspectivism. Dom Juan's failure shows that both the resistance to and overcoming of a patriarchal law are conditional on this perspectivism, on a rejection of gender binarism and that affirmative creation of new categories.

Indeed, this is a point that Kofman herself makes towards the end of the interview with which we began our discussion. There, she returns to this need to move beyond these categories:

> We have to try to think further, to invent other positions (. . .). We have to try to think in a different way than through the categories of the masculine and the feminine. (. . .). It is necessary to think completely differently. But how? In my

opinion, up until now, no one knows; that is not the last word, but only the first step. (QF, 73)

Here, I propose that we can take this as a continuation of her thinking of affirmative creation. Kofman acknowledges that this creation, or here 'invention', remains only the first step towards something new. Importantly, unlike Freud's 'first step', this effort involves not a disguised naturalism, but an explicit and open affirmation of a universal perspectivism. Once again, there is no explicit indication as to what form such creation or invention must take. However, in spite of the incomplete nature and cautious qualifications that Kofman adds to this suggestion, she is quite direct and explicit that moving beyond gender binarism forms a crucial part of this idea. Once again, as in her analysis of Dom Juan, gender categories of masculine/feminine or paternal/maternal are the main targets. In these texts, Kofman maintains that rather than enable or provide resources for creation, the maternal serves as a barrier. For Kofman, this affirmative creation is the first step beyond this gender binarism and towards a more just understanding of debt.

Conclusion

Far from a marginal text, 'L'art de ne pas payer ses dettes' should be understood as an important contribution to a substantial debate on law that occupies a prominent place in Kofman's philosophy. Rather than his successes, it is Dom Juan's failures which help connect Kofman's reading of Kant and Freud with the perspectivism of Nietzsche. We come to see that the maternal is far from an innocent category and that maternal authority and law does not offer an escape from patriarchy. The affirmative creation that Kofman suggests is precisely a question of disrupting and replacing such a category. Indeed, for Kofman, it is only in going beyond our current categories, including those of the paternal and maternal, that we can really arrive at an *art* of creating and affirming new and more just debts to one another.

ORCID

Cillian Ó Fathaigh https://orcid.org/0000-0002-7469-9403

NOTES

1 Sarah Kofman, 'La question des femmes: une impasse pour les philosophes', *Les Cahiers du GRIF* 46:1 (1992), 65–74 (70), hereafter QF. I am grateful to Jules Gawlik, Jasmine Cooper, Benjamin Dalton, Charlotte Thevenet and Luke Warde for their generous feedback on early drafts of this text, and to the Bill & Melinda Gates Foundation and the Gates Cambridge Trust for their financial support of this research (Grant Number: OPP1144). Unless otherwise indicated, all translations are my own.

2 Sarah Kofman, 'L'art de ne pas payer ses dettes' in *Don Juan ou le refus de la dette*, edited by Sarah Kofman and Jean-Yves Masson (Paris: Galilée, 1991), hereafter AP. The QF interview itself took place in the same year as this text was published.

3 Søren Kierkegaard, 'The Immediate Erotic Stages or the Musical Erotic' in *Either/Or*, translated by Alastair Hannay (London: Penguin, 1992 [1843]).

4 Sarah Kofman, 'Subvertir le philosophique ou Pour un supplément de jouissance' [interview with Evelyne Ender], *Compar(a)ison* 1 (1993), 9–26 (14), hereafter SP.

5 It is worth stressing that Kofman is not advocating a viewpoint, one we might suggest that is itself 'masculine', of total autonomy or indebtedness. As we see in our epigraph, Kofman does not appear to even consider this possible, let alone desirable.

6 Sarah Kofman, 'The Economy of Respect: Kant and Respect for Women', translated by Nicole Fisher, in *Selected Writings*, edited by Thomas Albrecht, with Georgia Albert and Elizabeth Rottenberg (Stanford, CA: Stanford University Press, 2007), hereafter ER.

7 Natalie Alexander, 'Rending Kant's Umbrella: Kofman's Diagnosis of Ethical Law' in *Enigmas: Essays on Sarah Kofman*, edited by Penelope Deutscher and Kelly Oliver (Ithaca, NY: Cornell University Press, 1998), 143–58 (158).

8 Sarah Kofman, 'Un autre Moïse, ou la Force de la loi' in *L'Imposture de la beauté et autres textes* (Paris: Galilée, 1995), hereafter AM.

9 This is also true of Kant's ambivalent position on the goddess Isis (ER, 198–9).

10 Sarah Kofman, *'Il n'y a que le premier pas qui coûte': Freud et la spéculation* (Paris: Galilée, 1991), 78, hereafter PC.

11 As we will see later, thought does seem to have an important position here, but it is also worth addressing the prominent position of sculpture in the texts here. Indeed, in Kofman's *Socrate(s)*, Kofman considers the importance of Socrates' father, Sophroniscus, being a sculptor. I am grateful to an anonymous reviewer for this rich suggestion.

12 Brian O'Keeffe, 'The Refusal of Debt: On Sarah Kofman's Version of Don Juan', *Symplokē* 25:1–2 (2017), 419–38 (436), hereafter RD.

13 Sarah Kofman, 'Baubô: Theological Perversion and Fetishism', translated by Tracy B. Strong, in *Feminist Interpretations of Friedrich Nietzsche*, edited by Kelly Oliver (University Park, PA: Pennsylvania State University Press, 1998), 21–49 (36), hereafter B.

14 Sarah Kofman, *Explosion II: les enfants de Nietzsche* (Galilée: Paris, 1993), 287, hereafter EX.

15 Sarah Kofman, *Camera Obscura: Of Ideology*, translated by Will Straw (Ithaca, NY: Cornell University Press, 1999), 43, hereafter CO.

16 Tina Chanter, 'Eating Words; Antigone as Kofman's Proper Name', 182, and Kelly Oliver, 'Sarah Kofman's Queasy Stomach and the Riddle of the Paternal Law', 198, in *Enigmas: Essays on Sarah Kofman*, edited by Penelope Deutscher and Kelly Oliver (Ithaca, NY: Cornell University Press, 1998), hereafter E.

17 Kelly Oliver, *Womanizing Nietzsche: Philosophy's Relation to the 'Feminine'* (New York: Routledge, 1995).

Of Metals and Men: Kofman, Conversion and *The Merchant of Venice*

Duncan Large

My focus in this article is on one of Sarah Kofman's less often studied texts, her extended essay on Freud's reading of Shakespeare's *The Merchant of Venice*, which was published in French in 1987 as a small book — *Conversions: 'Le Marchand de Venise' sous le signe de Saturne* (Conversions: *The Merchant of Venice* under the Sign of Saturn) — and in English translation (by Shaun Whiteside) three years later.[1] I will first examine *Conversions* as a response to a literary text, and consider the light it sheds on the relation between philosophy, psychoanalysis and literature in Kofman's work — for it is not just a reading of a literary text but a reading of a reading (by Freud), set off, as I shall argue, by a third interlocutor (Nietzsche). After setting out Freud's interpretation of *The Merchant of Venice*, then, and Kofman's response to it, I want to concentrate on Kofman's methodology and the crucial role played in *Conversions* by the concept of ambivalence. I will read this text as consonant with Kofman's career-long concern for tropes and metaphors, for transformations and metamorphoses — at the most basic level, how one thing turns into another — and argue that her ultimately intense deconstructive interest in ambivalence acts as a riposte to the binary logic of conversion that she sees at work all too often in Freud.

Kofman's short book is actually a critique of the notion of conversion, then, but beyond these initial frames of reference, in the latter half of the article I want to bring out three other kinds of conversion in Shakespeare's play which seem to me to be neglected by Kofman herself, and (in true Kofmanian fashion) subject these absences and aporias to my own symptomatic readings. I will read *Conversions* as an aspect of Kofman's increasing interest in the 1980s in Judaism, and in coming to terms with her own Jewishness: one of the

Paragraph 44.1 (2021): 26–40
DOI: 10.3366/para.2021.0352

www.euppublishing.com/para

conversions which Kofman thematizes is Shylock's forced conversion from Judaism to Christianity at the end of Act IV of Shakespeare's play, but I will be focusing on the other religious conversion in the play, which Kofman neglects, namely the unforced conversion of Shylock's daughter Jessica. That will inevitably bring me to an examination of some of the autobiographical elements which we can (and indeed are invited to) interpret *après coup* in the light of her late autobiographical text *Rue Ordener, rue Labat* (1994), specifically her own conversion to Christianity during World War II. I will also consider the theme of cross-dressing and gender fluidity in Shakespeare's text, which Kofman leaves surprisingly uncommented (given where the text comes in her oeuvre), and conclude by addressing one final supplementary sense of 'conversion', the question of translation.

'La relève de la philosophie'

Let me begin my analysis proper with a methodological reflection, by putting some linguistic pressure on the title of this collection: 'the relief of philosophy'. In (Derridean) French this formulation seems to me to describe rather well Kofman's attitude towards philosophy: 'la relève de la philosophie' or the sublation of philosophy. For Kofman philosophy is always destined to be sublated by literature and psychoanalysis: she holds the three in suspension, and they supplement each other. One could even go so far as to say 'ça relève de la philosophie' — it is in the nature of philosophy to be sublated. It is this approach that makes for the uncommon richness of Kofman's readings — advocating and demonstrating that the literary text has a truth of its own which is every bit as vital and urgent as the philosophical and psychoanalytic truths which it pre-empts. This, after all, is only what Freud himself maintained, in his letter to the great Viennese dramatist Arthur Schnitzler on the occasion of the latter's sixtieth birthday in 1922: 'I have formed the impression that you know through intuition — or rather from detailed self-observation — everything that I have discovered by laborious work on other people.'[2]

Kofman was writing on the intimate nexus between literature and philosophy right from her earliest publication (a 1963 article on Sartre).[3] Throughout her career she chose to work on literary philosophers and on philosophical literary writers, always scrupulous *not* to maintain a strict separation between the two categories. In her early publications of the 1970s she follows Freud's literary tastes in reading Freud's literary readings — a series of four essays which would become *Quatre romans analytiques* (1974) — and *Conversions* is clearly a pendant to that project (even if, as it happens, it was published in English in 1990, a year before Sarah Wykes's translation of *Quatre romans analytiques* as *Freud and Fiction*).[4] Kofman had not written on Shakespeare before this, and indeed she would not do so again: her interest is in Freud's reading, not so much in the Shakespeare itself, but in turn my interest will be in the interpretative gaps that inevitably result from such an approach.

Conversion and Ambivalence (Freud, Shakespeare, Nietzsche)

Kofman's essay is a reading of Freud's short piece 'Das Motiv der Kästchenwahl' (1913; literally 'The Motif of the Choice of Caskets', translated in the *Standard Edition* as 'The Theme of the Three Caskets').[5] Here Freud opens with a discussion of *The Merchant of Venice* and rapidly establishes a parallel with a second Shakespeare play, *King Lear*: one of the important sub-plots of *The Merchant of Venice* has Portia's suitors choosing between three caskets, and (once the caskets have been 'translated' by Freud into three women, by a process of 'symbolic substitution' (*symbolische Ersetzung*) (MK, 184/TT, 236)) this episode is paralleled with Lear choosing between his three daughters. In each case the least showy and apparently least valuable of the options is actually of the greatest value: in *The Merchant* it is the lead casket that contains the portrait of Portia, indicating a successful choice and her hand in marriage; in *King Lear* it is Cordelia whose mute love for Lear appears least but in fact is most fiercely sustained. Freud marshals a number of further examples from myth and fairy tales where a male character chooses between three women (for example, the Judgement of Paris, or 'Cinderella'), and isolates a common characteristic of muteness. He argues that the muteness of the chosen one indicates (by impeccable dream logic) that it (she) in fact symbolizes death, and the fact that the process is represented as an act of choice rather than an ineluctable necessity indicates for Freud a wish-fulfilment (as in a dream): such scenarios figure the desire to control one's own destiny, and the ultimate three women are indeed the Fates, who are depicted on the cover of the French edition of Kofman's text.

As Kofman points out (CF, 23/CE, 145), Freud reads these literary works as if they were dreams; in other words, his interpretation uses the binary logic of substitution and inversion (*Ersetzung* and *Umkehrung* are the key operative terms in the text).[6] Freudian dream logic is a logic of transformations, whereby one thing turns into another (its opposite), one thing can be translated into another in an interpretation which unfolds according to a principle of strict one-to-one equivalence. Thus in Shakespeare's text (on Freud's reading, according to Kofman) the first substitution is the claim that the three caskets stand for three women (hence the parallel with *Lear*), but Freud in fact makes a chain of substitutions, of which this is only the first: the lead casket signifies the pale, mute woman, who in turn signifies death; as in medieval alchemy, lead is but the point of departure for a series of transformations (CF, 44/CE, 152).

But Kofman highlights an important and under-recognized feature of Freud's analysis: there is a point in Freud's narrative where the binary dream logic of inversion and substitution gives way to the recognition of 'an ancient ambivalence' of meaning (MK, 191/TT, 244), between love and death (as two sides of the same coin). It is not that one turns into the other, he argues, but that both are available at the same time, and he points out the historic identity between different guises of Aphrodite: the goddess of love is *also* the bringer of death. So in this case the process of conversion is incomplete because the one has not been transformed into the other wholly and without residue. Instead of a straight 'replacement by the opposite' (*Ersetzung durch das Gegenteil*) (MK, 190/TT, 244), the 'opposite' origin remains, at least in trace form, and gives itself away to the trained hermeneut who knows where to look: 'On closer inspection we observe, to be sure, that the original myth is not so thoroughly distorted that traces of it (*Resterscheinungen*) do not show through and betray its presence' (MK, 191/TT, 245).

Although Kofman does not establish the parallel, this is actually (also) a Nietzschean gesture. Just as Freud is interested in the alchemical process of dream/myth interpretation and of literary symbolism, whereby something stands for and needs to be interpreted as its opposite, so Nietzsche is also drawn to the alchemical, to the conversion of base metal into gold, in the context of values. He opens his 1878 text *Human, All Too Human* with a 'chemistry of concepts and sensations', arguing:

> Historical philosophy, by contrast (. . .), has ascertained (. . .) that there are no opposites (. . .): according to its explanation, there are, strictly speaking, neither any unegoistical actions nor any completely disinterested contemplation; both are only sublimations (*Sublimirungen*), in which the fundamental element appears to

have almost evaporated (*fast verflüchtigt erscheint*) and reveals its presence only to the keenest observation.[7]

Kofman explicitly criticizes Freud for a failure to see the importance of this kind of ambivalence in Shakespeare's text: 'Freud's error', she writes (CF, 41/CE, 151), is that he is led astray by the dream logic of inversion to focus exclusively on the lead casket (which he wants to ally with the goddess of death) and to ignore the lesson of the ambivalence of *all* the metals:

> Thus, gold, silver and lead are all ambivalent, with an ambivalence that is concealed by their being split into three different, even opposite metals, which disguises their profound kinship, their common derivation from the metal which is supposed to be the most base: lead or Saturn; a split which masks the fact that each of them, and not lead alone, secretes (*porte inscrit en lui*) time, the risk of transformation, of deterioration, of transmutation in one direction or the other, and conceals, beneath gilded and silvered surfaces, genesis, development (*le devenir*) and death. (CF, 46/CE, 153)

Shaun Whiteside's English translation of 'le devenir' in the final sentence as 'development' rather than 'becoming' conceals the Nietzschean coordinates of Kofman's analysis; elsewhere, for example, she refers explicitly to Shylock's 'will to power' (CF, 66/CE, 161). In *Conversions* Kofman applies a Nietzsche-derived corrective to Freud — and appropriately enough Whiteside would go on to translate Nietzsche's *The Birth of Tragedy* for Penguin Classics three years later.[8]

For Kofman's hermeneutics, then, the concept of ambivalence is crucial and supersedes (dare one say, sublates) the various conversions on which Freud concentrates.[9] Conversion is usually associated with a Damascene moment of *anagnorisis* (recognition) and *peripeteia* (sudden reversal of fortune — of the kind that befalls Shakespeare's merchant of Venice, Antonio, no less than twice in the course of the play), where scales fall from eyes and one thing flips or converts into another. Conversion is often accompanied by a violence: a developing situation reaches a tipping point, then switches in a catastrophic event — and indeed on the back cover of the French edition of *Conversions* Kofman glosses 'conversion' as 'catastrophic reversal'[10] (cf. CF, 43/CE, 152). In the process of conversion, one thing wholly becomes another, stands for the other and takes its place, entirely occluding it. But the message of ambivalence is that no successful, complete, perfective conversion is possible. The two obey differing logics: on the one hand, Freud's binary logic of either/or; on the other, Kofman's deconstructive post-binary logic of both/and. In turn, Kofman herself proceeds to generalize the category of ambivalence and apply it to the rest of the play's themes in a chapter, 'Towards a General Ambivalence', that takes up over half of her text (CF, 31–70). Such a generalized theory of ambivalence is characterized by situations where two mutually antagonistic meanings exist simultaneously, one always poised to turn into the other on the stroke of an interpretation, like a semiotic Schrödinger's cat (conversion is an activity, ambivalence is a state awaiting an interpretation).[11]

Kofman's argument reaches its culmination in her characterization of 'the structural ambivalence of time' itself: 'With and through time, which is fundamentally ambivalent, all conversions remain possible' (CF, 54/CE, 156). This is what Kofman calls the 'true "theme" of this baroque drama' (back cover; cf. CF, 68/CE, 161). It is not the first time that Kofman has made the notion of ambivalence work this hard: it is crucial to her reading of Freud's texts on E. T. A. Hoffmann too, for example,[12] and — incarnated in the recurring figure of the Janus face — it is an important feature of her analysis of Freud's book on jokes, of Nietzsche's autobiography *Ecce homo*, and so forth.[13] In the conclusion to *Conversions* her claim is that the generalization of ambivalence (dis)qualifies Freud's overly simplistic readings of literature based on dream interpretations which in turn hinge on one-for-one decipherings. Kofman is presenting an alternative hermeneutics: she is correcting 'Freud's error' not only in his reading of this play but in his reading of fiction more generally. One might say that Kofman converts conversion into ambivalence (and she argues that Freud missed a trick by not doing so himself), or that conversion is sublated by ambivalence.

Jessica and Sarah

At this point, though, one is entitled to feel slightly puzzled by the title of Kofman's work. Specifically: if ambivalence sublates (*relève*) conversion as an interpretative category, why does the book highlight the term to such an extent? After all, *The Merchant of Venice* is described by Kofman as 'a drama of conversion in all its forms' (CF, 68f./CE, 162). Now we need to bear in mind that 'Conversions' is Kofman's word, not Freud's, and she has chosen a particularly polysemous word to summarize all the different kinds of transformation that she is interested in, in Shakespeare's play and Freud's reading of it. The

German translation of her text is titled *Konversionen* (1989),[14] but that is not a term that Freud himself uses in his essay — as mentioned above, Freud predominantly uses the terms *Ersetzung* and *Umkehrung*, meaning respectively substitution and *in*version. The dictionary offers many other possible German terms for 'conversion', most of which are formed with the prefix '*Um*' — *Umrechnung, Umsetzung, Umbau, Umstellung, Umwandlung, Umformung, Umwechslung, Umdeutung* — but Freud does not use any of these in his essay. Nor indeed does Freud use the more standard word for religious conversion in German, *Bekehrung*, which is used by August Wilhelm von Schlegel in the standard German translated edition of the play, at the only point in Shakespeare's text when religious 'conversion' is explicitly mentioned, by Shylock's daughter Jessica in III.5:

> Nay, you need not fear us, Lorenzo. Launcelot and I are out. He tells me flatly there's no mercy for me in heaven because I am a Jew's daughter, and he says you are no good member of the commonwealth, for in converting Jews to Christians, you raise the price of pork. (Shakespeare, *The Merchant of Venice*, III.5.25–9)[15]

> Ihr habt nichts zu befürchten, Lorenzo; Lanzelot und ich, wir sind ganz entzweit. Er sagt mir grade heraus, im Himmel sei keine Gnade für mich, weil ich eines Juden Tochter bin; und er behauptet, daß Ihr kein gutes Mitglied des gemeinen Wesens seid, weil Ihr Juden zum Christentum bekehrt und dadurch den Preis des Schweinefleisches steigert.[16]

By highlighting 'conversion' in her title, and using a word, '*Conversions*', which allows (more easily than in German) a parallel to be established between religious conversion and other kinds, Kofman draws greater attention than otherwise to, precisely, the religious connotation of conversion (and she certainly makes more of the theme than does Freud, who ignores the religious dimension of Shakespeare's play entirely in his 1913 treatment and makes no mention of either Shylock or Jessica). This in turn marks a new direction in Kofman's writings of the 1980s and 1990s, a reflection on Judaism and the Holocaust (the other main text which she published in 1987 was her first significant text on a Jewish theme, *Smothered Words* (*Paroles suffoquées*)).[17] Now Kofman supplements Freud's interpretation of Shakespeare's text by pointing out that, as she puts it on the back cover, 'the conversion of the Jew is merely a specific case of a general, reciprocal convertibility (of the characters Antonio, Bassanio, Shylock and the metals they represent, lead, gold, silver).' Kofman's book generalizes conversion, then, and extrapolates it from the religious variety, but I want to bring Kofman back to the religious theme, and focus in particular not on the forced conversion of Shylock but on the conversion of Shylock's daughter Jessica in the play.

In *Conversions*, Kofman focuses exclusively on Shylock's conversion (CF, 67/CE, 161) and fails to thematize his daughter Jessica, who also converts. There are important differences between the fates of the two characters: in IV.1 Shylock is obliged by Antonio to agree to be forcibly converted as punishment for insisting on his bond — a 'conversion stipulation' (in the words of Joan Ozark Holmer) that is peculiar to Shakespeare's version of the story and is not present in his source material.[18] Jessica, on the other hand, willingly agrees to convert (and abjure her Judaism) through marriage to the Christian Lorenzo. Jessica is converted through marriage, and as Holmer points out, Shakespeare presumably invents the name Jessica in the first place, with its allusion to the biblical figure of Jesse, precisely in order to (silently) invoke a biblical figure who is a willing convert to Christianity.[19] Jessica elopes with Lorenzo, taking with her a large cache of her father's jewels: she 'steal[s] from the wealthy Jew' (V.1.15) in all senses, and in this respect the play is a tale of multiple faithlessness.

The only point in Kofman's text where Jessica is mentioned is in the context of her theft of the jewels (CF, 61/CE, 159). I want to argue that Kofman's omission of Jessica otherwise is a blind spot that betrays an anxiety stemming from an uneasy identification with Shakespeare's character. After all, the play has a very real personal connection for her if we bear in mind that Freud cites it according to its standard German title of *Der Kaufmann von Venedig*.[20] Kofman's significant personal investment in her analysis of Freud's reading of the play becomes apparent if we read it in the context of the culmination of that autobiographical strain in her writing which is *Rue Ordener, rue Labat* (1994). This is the text that reveals that for Kofman there is a very personal relation to 'conversion' in the religious sense because during the war she converted to Christianity herself. At the opening of *Rue Ordener* she invites us to read her earlier works in the light of it, so that is what I will briefly now do: 'Maybe all my books have been the detours required to bring me to write about "that".'[21]

Her father Bereck Kofman acts as a kind of patron for *Rue Ordener* since he is invoked right at the outset in the form of his old fountain pen which, we are told, constrains her to write. We have seen that Kofman has no compunction about criticizing her mentor and 'setting Freud straight' in her analysis of his reading of Shakespeare, but the memory of her actual father (murdered in Auschwitz) is steadfastly and faithfully cultivated. Things are very different with her mother, though, and the main narrative in *Rue Ordener, rue Labat* concerns how she turned against her birth mother in favour of her adoptive mother Mémé in wartime Paris. She relates how she begins to eat pork and forgets her Yiddish; she is baptized and passes as Mémé's daughter, willingly taking on the name Suzanne. She internalizes Mémé's anti-Semitism and begins to hate her own Jewishness. In her repudiation of Judaism Sarah/Suzanne resembles Shakespeare's Jessica, the willing convert. Yet her attitude to her two mothers is agonal, ambivalent, and defies Jessica's binary logic. Paradoxically, Mémé makes her more conscious than ever of her Judaism — by, for example, introducing her to Jewish thinkers such as Spinoza, Bergson, Einstein and Marx — then after the war Sarah reclaims her Jewish inheritance, vindicating the fears of Shakespeare's contemporary audience that the Jewish daughter's conversion to Christianity might not last.[22] I agree here with Joanne Faulkner, who argues 'that Kofman's abjection of Judaism is crucial to the construction of her Jewish identity in the context of the Nazi occupation — that at the heart of all identification is ambivalence'.[23]

'Turn[ing] to men'

Such neglect of the character of Jessica is also one aspect of how very little Kofman remarks on the women in Shakespeare's text, despite the fact that *Conversions* postdates her main groundbreaking work in feminist criticism — from 'Baubô' (1975) through *The Enigma of Woman* (1980) to *Le Respect des femmes* (The Respect of Women) (1982).[24] The final aspect of the 'conversion' theme I want to explore here is another that Kofman herself neglects, namely the various ways in which Shakespeare's female characters are converted into men. The theme of the Saturnalia interested Kofman as early as *Nietzsche and Metaphor*,[25] and not surprisingly it is also discussed in *Conversions:* The Merchant of Venice *under the Sign of Saturn* (CF, 65–7/CE, 160f.), but one important aspect of this feature of Elizabethan life as depicted in Shakespeare is the saturnalia of gender. Of course, female characters were played by male actors in the first place, but this was compounded by further cross-dressing.[26]

In *The Merchant of Venice*, Jessica's first conversion is actually in II.6, when she is 'transformèd to a boy' (II.6.40) in order to escape from her father's supervision and elope. When it comes to transforming and converting herself, then, Jessica is like Homer's Odysseus, 'much-turned' (πολύτροπον). Jessica's travesty in II.6 then establishes the precedent for the rather better-known cross-dressing episode in IV.1, when Nerissa and Portia 'turn to men' (III.4.78) to become the lawyers for the trial scene. But there is a chiastic structure here because just as Jessica prefigures Portia's transformation, Portia returns the compliment with a dress rehearsal for Jessica's conversion-by-marriage in III.1. Portia is indeed the first character to be converted in the play, for after Bassanio correctly chooses the lead casket, Portia tells him: 'Myself and what is mine, to you and yours / Is now converted' (III.2.166–7). Portia seals this conversion by giving Bassanio the ring which he will subsequently give to 'Balthazar' in IV.2, only for the latter to return the ring in V.1 having converted back to Portia. In the world of Elizabethan comedy the conversion of cross-dressing is bound to be temporary and undone before the close, but as Holmer points out, these transformations can never be entirely undone since 'Jessica, Portia, and Nerissa all have names that are feminine conversions of masculine names so that all three women "turn to men" (III.4.78) in names as well as cross-gendered disguise.'[27] Such conversions are revealed to be but impermanent, reversible oscillations, which suggests the model of ambivalence rather than conversion once again.

Conclusion: 'this conversion that is called translation'

Kofman's critical reading of Freud's interpretation of Shakespeare sublates multiple instances of conversion, converting them into so many kinds of ambivalence, and I have supplemented Kofman's account by extending the reach of her model of ambivalence to cover a number of other kinds of conversion in *The Merchant of Venice* which Kofman and Freud both neglect. In conclusion, though, I want to ask what might be the implications of the general theory of ambivalence that Kofman sets out for what Derrida refers to as 'this conversion that is called translation'.[28]

Kofman's biographer Karoline Feyertag argues that 'Without doubt the concept of translation is central to her thinking.'[29] Christie McDonald figures Kofman's wartime conversion as a 'self-translation',[30] and Kofman figures herself as a translator (of Kafka) in the dream which she reports and analyses in the short 1976 text 'Tomb for a Proper Name'.[31] She took a keen interest in translations of her work and was very supportive of her translators, while in the works themselves, although she always gives original-language quotations where necessary for the purposes of her argument, she also cites an array of translations. In *Conversions* the first point that Kofman makes is about a translation: in her first footnote she criticizes translator Marie Bonaparte's French title for Freud's text ('Le thème des trois coffrets' rather than 'Le motif du choix des coffrets' — CF, 11n. 1/CE, 162n. 1).[32] But that initial comment is the only explicit reference to translation in Kofman's text, which refuses to describe as a translation any of the conversions, inversions, replacements, exchanges, metaphorical substitutions, transformations or transmutations which it otherwise identifies in Shakespeare's play. A decade after Kofman, Derrida will have no such qualms, claiming in his 1998 lecture 'What is a "Relevant" Translation?' that 'everything in the play can be retranslated into the code of translation and as a problem of translation' (QTR, 30/WRT, 372). He proceeds to read the play as a *locus classicus* of translation motifs, going so far as to claim (without reference to Kofman's study) that 'all translation is a conversion' (QTR, 31/WRT, 373),[33] and his English translator Lawrence Venuti then ensures that the lecture (and its reading of *The Merchant of Venice*) becomes a classic of translation studies by including his own translation in his best-selling *Translation Studies Reader*.

Unlike Derrida, Kofman did not write extensively on translation, and even *Conversions*, with its concern for all kinds of transformation, only points towards what a Kofmanian theory of translation would look like, but she is at least more explicit elsewhere. One of the most substantial comments that Kofman makes on translation comes in *Comment s'en sortir?* ('Beyond Aporia?') (1983), when she is writing of the ambiguities of the word 'poros' in relation to translating it:

> To translate, to open up a path through a language by using its resources, to decide upon *one* meaning, is to escape the agonizing, aporetic impasses of any translation, to make the philosophical gesture *par excellence*: the gesture of betrayal (*un geste de trahison*). To recognize the untranslatability of *poros* and *aporia* is to indicate that there is something about the terms, which Plato borrows from a whole tradition, which breaks with a philosophical conception of translation, and with the logic of identity that it implies.[34]

Following Walter Benjamin, Kofman is critical of the standard model of translation as conversion between equivalents, just as she is critical of Freudian dream theory for the same reason: 'traditional' translation for Kofman is a betrayal.[35] The translator is faced with an array of choices and usually needs to plump for one or the other. In the case of highly polysemous terms like *poros* and *aporia* it is obvious that limiting the range of signification promotes loss and amounts to a betrayal, but in fact this is the case to a greater or lesser extent in all acts of translation. The alternative is to embrace at least a degree of untranslatability in every translation, to hold open ambiguity and prize ambivalence (the logic of the both/and). Most publishers would not look kindly on a translator who submitted final copy offering a wealth of unresolved alternatives, but it ought at least to be possible to treat the untranslatable as a kind of regulative idea. This is the position — of studied ambivalence — adopted by Barbara Cassin for her monumental project the *Dictionary of Untranslatables*, which defines its subject, and its approach, with the watchword: 'the untranslatable is rather what one keeps on (not) translating'.[36] In adopting a theory of translation based not on equivalence but on ambivalence in this way, Cassin seems to me to be Kofman's worthy successor.

ORCID

Duncan Large https://orcid.org/0000-0001-6555-7334

NOTES

1 Sarah Kofman, *Conversions: 'Le Marchand de Venise' sous le signe de Saturne* (Paris: Galilée, 1987), hereafter CF; Sarah Kofman, 'Conversions: *The Merchant of Venice* under the Sign of Saturn', translated by Shaun Whiteside, in *Literary Theory Today*, edited by Peter Collier and Helga Geyer–Ryan (Cambridge: Polity Press, 1990), 142–66, hereafter CE.

2 Sigmund Freud, *Letters of Sigmund Freud*, translated by Tania and James Stern, edited by Ernst L. Freud (New York: Basic Books, 1960), 339f.; Sigmund Freud, *Briefe 1873–1939*, edited by Ernst L. Freud (Frankfurt am Main: Fischer, 1960), 249f.

3 Sarah Kofman, 'Le problème moral dans une philosophie de l'absurde', *Revue de l'enseignement philosophique* 14:1 (1963), 1–7; reprinted in Sarah Kofman, *Séductions: De Sartre à Héraclite* (Paris: Galilée, 1990), 167–81.

4 Sarah Kofman, *Quatre romans analytiques* (Paris: Galilée, 1974); translated by Sarah Wykes as *Freud and Fiction* (Boston, MA: Northeastern University Press; Cambridge: Polity Press, 1991).

5 Sigmund Freud, 'Das Motiv der Kästchenwahl' in *Studienausgabe*, edited by Alexander Mitscherlich, Angela Richards and James Strachey (Frankfurt am Main: Fischer, 2000), X, 181–93, hereafter MK; Sigmund Freud, 'The Theme of the Three Caskets', translated by C. J. M. Hubback, in *Art and*

Literature (Penguin Freud Library, volume XIV), edited by Albert Dickson (London: Penguin, 1990), 233–47, hereafter TT.

6 Graham Frankland suggests an important qualification: 'Rather than reducing literature to the status of a dream, Freud seems, rightly or wrongly, to *elevate* the dream to the status of literary text.' Graham Frankland, *Freud's Literary Culture* (Cambridge: Cambridge University Press, 2000), 133.

7 Friedrich Nietzsche, *Human, All Too Human, I*, translated by Gary Handwerk, in *Complete Works*, edited by Bernd Magnus (Stanford, CA: Stanford University Press, 1995), 3, 15; Friedrich Nietzsche, *Menschliches, Allzumenschliches*, I, 1, in *Kritische Studienausgabe*, edited by Giorgio Colli and Mazzino Montinari, 15 volumes, 2nd edition (Munich: dtv, 1988), 2, 23f. Kofman cites §162 of the same text in a footnote elsewhere (CF, 42n. 5).

8 Friedrich Nietzsche, *The Birth of Tragedy out of the Spirit of Music*, translated by Shaun Whiteside, edited by Michael Tanner (London and New York: Penguin, 1993).

9 Harold Bloom, likewise, stresses the importance of ambivalence in the play. See Harold Bloom, *Shakespeare: The Invention of the Human* (New York: Riverhead Books, 1998), 189f.

10 Where not otherwise indicated, translations are my own.

11 Also of relevance here is the notion of 'convertibility' that Jean Emily Tan derives from her reading of Kofman's contemporaneous text *Paroles suffoquées* (Smothered Words). See Jean Emily Tan, 'Sarah Kofman as Philosopher of the Uncanny Double: Sarah Kofman's Appropriation of Nietzsche and Freud' (unpublished PhD dissertation, Loyola University Chicago, 2009), 226–9.

12 See Duncan Large, 'Kofman's Hoffmann' in *Enigmas: Essays on Sarah Kofman*, edited by Penelope Deutscher and Kelly Oliver (Ithaca, NY and London: Cornell University Press, 1999), 67–83 and 242–5.

13 See Sarah Kofman, 'Un Janus double face' in *Pourquoi rit–on? Freud et le mot d'esprit* (Paris: Galilée, 1986), 74–82 and *Explosion I: de l''Ecce Homo' de Nietzsche* (Paris: Galilée, 1992), 157.

14 Sarah Kofman, *Konversionen: Der Kaufmann von Venedig unter dem Zeichen des Saturn*, edited by Peter Engelmann, translated by Monika Buchgeister (Vienna: Passagen, 1989).

15 *The Merchant of Venice* is cited in the New Cambridge Shakespeare edition by M. M. Mahood, 3rd edition (Cambridge: Cambridge University Press, 2018).

16 William Shakespeare, *Sämtliche Werke*, edited by Erich Loewenthal, 4 volumes, 5th edition (Heidelberg: Lambert Schneider, 1987), *I: Komödien*, 613.

17 Sarah Kofman, *Paroles suffoquées* (Paris: Galilée, 1987); translated by Madeleine Dobie as *Smothered Words* (Evanston, IL: Northwestern University Press, 1998).

18 Joan Ozark Holmer, *The Merchant of Venice: Choice, Hazard and Consequence* (Basingstoke and London: Macmillan, 1995), 221. See also Kenneth Gross, *Shylock is Shakespeare* (Chicago and London: University of Chicago Press, 2006), 107, and Bloom, *Shakespeare*, 191.

19 See Holmer, *The Merchant of Venice*, 86.

20 Shakespeare's Kaufmann/Kofman is of course Antonio, not Shylock, although Portia's Doctor Balthazar, at least, cannot initially tell them apart (IV.1.170: 'Which is the merchant here and which the Jew?'). On their confusing similarities, see, for example, Graham Holderness, *The Merchant of Venice* (London: Penguin, 1993), 24–8. On the etymology of Kofman's surname, see Sarah Kofman, 'Trois textes autobiographiques', *La Part de l'oeil* 9 (1993), 83–5 (84); translated by Frances Bartkowski and Georgia Albert as 'Tomb for a Proper Name' in Sarah Kofman, *Selected Writings*, edited by Thomas Albrecht, with Georgia Albert and Elizabeth Rottenberg (Stanford, CA: Stanford University Press, 2007), 248–9.

21 Sarah Kofman, *Rue Ordener, rue Labat* (Paris: Galilée, 1994), 9, and Sarah Kofman, *Rue Ordener, Rue Labat*, translated by Ann Smock (Lincoln, NE: University of Nebraska Press, 1996), 3, hereafter RO; page numbers are to the French-language edition followed by the English-language edition.

22 RO, 57/47. On fears that Jessica's 'blood' would win out, see James Shapiro, *Shakespeare and the Jews*, 2nd edition (New York: Columbia University Press, 2016), 158f., Janet Adelman, 'Her Father's Blood: Conversion, Race, and Nation' in *Blood Relations: Christian and Jew in 'The Merchant of Venice'* (Chicago and London: University of Chicago Press, 2008), 66–98, and Brett D. Hirsch, 'Counterfeit Professions: Jewish Daughters and the Drama of Failed Conversion in Marlowe's *The Jew of Malta* and Shakespeare's *The Merchant of Venice*', *Early Modern Literary Studies* Special Issue 19 (2009), 4.1–37, http://purl.oclc.org/emls/si-19/hirscoun.html.

23 Joanne Faulkner, '"Keeping It in the Family": Sarah Kofman Reading Nietzsche as a Jewish Woman', *Hypatia* 23:1 (2008), 41–64 (42). See also Karoline Feyertag, *Sarah Kofman: Eine Biographie* (Vienna and Berlin: Turia + Kant, 2014), 269–80.

24 See Sarah Kofman, 'Baubô: Theological Perversion and Fetishism', translated by Tracy B. Strong, in *Feminist Interpretations of Friedrich Nietzsche*, edited by Kelly Oliver (University Park, PA: Pennsylvania State University Press, 1998), 21–49, *The Enigma of Woman: Woman in Freud's Writings*, translated by Catherine Porter (Ithaca, NY: Cornell University Press, 1985), and *Le Respect des femmes (Kant et Rousseau)* (Paris: Galilée, 1982).

25 See Sarah Kofman, 'Les Saturnales' in *Nietzsche et la métaphore*, 2nd edition (Paris: Galilée, 1983), 106–17, and 'Saturnalia' in *Nietzsche and Metaphor*,

translated by Duncan Large (London: Athlone Press; Stanford, CA: Stanford University Press, 1993), 74–80.

26 For a detailed discussion of this theme in the play, see Michael Shapiro, *Gender in Play on the Shakespearean Stage: Boy Heroines and Female Pages* (Ann Arbor, MI: University of Michigan Press, 1994), 97–113.

27 Holmer, *The Merchant of Venice*, 88.

28 Jacques Derrida, 'Qu'est-ce qu'une traduction "relevante"?' in *Actes des quinzièmes assises de la traduction littéraire (Arles 1998)* (Arles: Actes Sud, 1999), 21–48 (31), hereafter QTR; Jacques Derrida, 'What is a "Relevant" Translation?', translated by Lawrence Venuti, in *The Translation Studies Reader*, edited by Venuti, 3rd edition (London and New York: Routledge, 2012), 365–88 (373), hereafter WRT.

29 Feyertag, *Sarah Kofman*, 260.

30 Christie McDonald, 'Sarah Kofman: Effecting Self Translation', *TTR: traduction, terminologie, rédaction* 11:2 (1998), 185–97.

31 Kofman, 'Trois textes autobiographiques', 84; Kofman, 'Tomb for a Proper Name', 248.

32 It should be noted that Kofman has by this stage (the second line of her text) already mis-cited the German title of Freud's essay (as 'Das Motiv der Kästenwahl' rather than 'Kästchenwahl' (CF, 11)); later, perhaps under pressure from the Bonaparte translation, she also mis-cites the title in French as '*[Le] Motif du choix des trois coffrets*' (CF, 26). Freud himself grumbles in one of his footnotes that the Schlegel translation of *King Lear* misses Cordelia's muteness (MK, 186n. 2/TT, 239n. 1).

33 On the relation between Jewish–Christian conversion and translation, see especially Naomi Seidman, 'False Friends: Conversion and Translation from Jerome to Luther' in *Faithful Renderings: Jewish–Christian Difference and the Politics of Translation* (Chicago and London: University of Chicago Press, 2006), 115–52.

34 Sarah Kofman, *Comment s'en sortir?* (Paris: Galilée, 1983), 17f.; Sarah Kofman, 'Beyond Aporia?', translated by David Macey, in *Post-structuralist Classics*, edited by Andrew Benjamin (London and New York: Routledge, 1988), 7–44 (9f.).

35 See also Kofman, 'Traduttore, traditore' in *Pourquoi rit-on?*, 59–92 (especially 72–4). On psychoanalysis as a form of translation, see Alan Bass, 'On the History of a Mistranslation and the Psychoanalytic Movement' in *Difference in Translation*, edited by Joseph F. Graham (Ithaca, NY and London: Cornell University Press, 1985), 102–41 (especially 102–4).

36 Barbara Cassin, 'Introduction' in *Dictionary of Untranslatables: A Philosophical Lexicon*, edited by Cassin, translated by Steven Rendall et al. (Princeton, NJ and Oxford: Princeton University Press, 2014), xvii.

Reading Derrida Reading Kofman

GINETTE MICHAUD

> Finishing this book today, September 25, the day of Yom Kippur, I cannot resist peddling this Jewish joke told by Theodor Reik: 'Two Jews, long-standing enemies, meet at the synagogue on the day of the Great Atonement. One says to the other: 'I wish you what you wish me.' And the other replies, giving tit for tat: 'See, you're doing it again!'
> In conclusion, let us leave the last word to laughter.[1]
>
> Sarah Kofman, *Pourquoi rit-on?* (Why Do People Laugh?)

> So what then? Let read, if at all possible, if the other can... the other who comes after... let them live.
>
> Jacques Derrida, '.......', *Les Cahiers du Grif* (164)

Before examining some of the traces left behind by Jacques Derrida's relationship with Sarah Kofman's work, I would like to let her speak, thus giving her precedence in these exchanges, which she was the first to impel by way of her book *Lectures de Derrida* (Readings of Derrida), published in 1984, but whose centrepieces had appeared earlier, in 1973 (for 'Un philosophe "unheimlich"' (An 'Unheimlich' Philosopher)) and 1981 (for 'Ça cloche', an insightful reading of *Glas*).[2]

Kofman unrelentingly stressed that she was not a 'student' of Derrida's, and that he could not act as her master or as a father figure, but at best as a brother (although one should reread what Derrida has written on brotherhood, especially as regards the role of the sister in *Politics of Friendship*). In an article entitled 'Pardon: Sarah Kofman and Jacques Derrida', Penelope Deutscher suggests that

Paragraph 44.1 (2021): 41–57
DOI: 10.3366/para.2021.0353

www.euppublishing.com/para

Derrida acknowledges Kofman's readings of Nietzsche only tacitly in his book:

> Taking seriously the suggestion that one can usefully reflect on Derrida and Kofman's relationship in terms of the structure of the debt, we can revisit their reading of Nietzsche, and of friendship (...). So when Derrida taxes Nietzsche with his fraternal metaphor, and includes a long discussion of Kofman's famous thematic, respect for women in Kant, perhaps he is sending greetings to Kofman.[3]

According to the Derridean logic of the debt and the gift, every offering must remain 'oblique' if it is to escape the economic circuit of exchange and truly be welcomed as a gift, which implies that the offering must be made unbeknownst to the giver and the beneficiary (a topic to which I shall return).

In any case, when Kofman published her book on Derrida in 1984, she already had several monographs to her name — she shows herself to be supremely sensitive to the question of appropriative mastery. Lucidly emphasizing the pitfalls she will avoid — 'writing a thesis on Derrida is out of the question. Both today and tomorrow' (L, 15) — she derides any and all genealogical, historical or dialectically minded approaches that claim to grasp such a body of work (Derrida's, but also her own), work 'that can no longer be understood as the linear (...) development of an initial kernel' (L, 32). From the outset, Kofman is convinced that, in accordance with the 'Strange structure of the supplement, which belatedly produces that to which it supposedly adds (...) [, w]hat seems to be on the fringes of the body proper, what lies below or is ultimately rejected, and which opens unto the outside, is sometimes more important than the so-called main text' (L, 17).[4] These are principles of reading that underpin her work in its entirety, where it is always the detail that matters, that 'makes the difference', as she puts it.[5] Thus, she chooses to 'read obliquely' (L, 33) for the sake of a deliberate practice of reading as generalized grafting, since 'More than the content of thoughts or their evolution, it is the way texts are made, play, are written, that Derrida questions' (L, 46): 'This allows us to understand that under no circumstances can a graft, no matter how inevitable, be favoured or act as a frame' (L, 54).

In rereading this piece, which prefigures many later developments, one is struck by the audacity of Kofman's blunt wording. Regarding 'the voice [that] alone seems to accomplish the origin's circular return to itself', she pithily comments as follows: 'self-fellatio, self-insemination' (L, 29). In an equally incisive manner, she grants her full attention to appendices and postscripts, 'previously considered excrements' (L, 98), as she puts it. Not only does she see that 'Derridean undecidables are all playing with the death they carry "within"' (L, 89), she foregrounds this Derridean law, which also happens to be her own:

> Derrida (. . .). does not seek to determine the law that governs internal conflicts; rather, he focuses on the *internal* conflicts of texts, their heterogeneity and their contradictions. He aims to rigorously articulate the text of life and the text of writing. (. . .) This is a reading that rests on the distinction between *doing* and *saying*, between what is *written* and *said*, between *description* and *declaration*. (L, 104)

Better yet, one is struck by two statements that perceptively underscore (1) the importance of sexual difference in Derrida's thought (L, 113); (2) the question of parricide and its impact (L, 114). What is more, one of the most substantial advancements of these *Lectures de Derrida* can be seen in the fact that Kofman chooses, in this piece (and we must not forget that it was written in 1973) 'Sexual violence, the difference between the sexes [as the] best paradigm for *différance*' (L, 69), thus making room for psychoanalysis and for the debate that ties it to deconstruction.

Yet this boldness has not prevented some critics from placing Kofman back under Derrida's authority, since he was the 'father' of deconstruction (an expression that speaks volumes about their misunderstanding of 'deconstruction', both word and thing). Even were we to assume that Kofman 'is simply "an orthodox Derridean"', casting her in this role would be far from simple (and 'who is to say who is debtor and indebted in a master–disciple relationship?' (PS, 26), as Deutscher aptly asks). Even as Kofman tirelessly draws our attention, in her readings of Derrida's texts, to the alertness required when dealing with questions of mastery and appropriation, these texts which are shown to have become sites of porousness and contamination, too many readers apply the very treatment she carefully picks apart to her own work! They fail to take her own strategy of citation and textual grafting into account, which is an *original* means of criticizing any and all positions of authorship and authority, a way of speaking into the mask, much like Echo, albeit in her own name. For what is interesting in this Kofmanian reading is not so much its penchant for symbiosis and 'hysterical' identification with the corpus she analyses; nor is it her singular practice of citation, which she pushes to the limit in this piece and everywhere else. Rather, it is her ability to reconcile what seems utterly contradictory: making her voice heard through that of the other, marking her closeness to the other even as she widens a gap that is irreducible to appropriation.

★

What goes on between Kofman and Derrida? Between Derrida and Kofman? It may no longer be the 'same thing', once we have inverted these two names between which no symmetry ought to be assumed. There is no simple or obvious 'reciprocity' here, aside from the fact that there is a book (Kofman's) and a substantial essay (Derrida's), as well as several references and quotations on both parts. That said, these traces are more plentiful on Kofman's part, whereas there are several notorious omissions on Derrida's, inasmuch as he does not recall Kofman's work as often as one would expect. The edited volume to which they both contributed, *Mimesis des articulations* (Mimesis: [Dis]articulations)[6] ('our shared child' [*notre enfant communautaire*][7] as Kofman likes to call it) is the most obvious sign of this. However, other decisive topics spring to mind — the two thinkers' 'readings of woman as veil and enigma in Nietzsche', of 'castration anxiety and fetishism in Freud' (PS, 26), of representation and imitation, metaphor, autobiographical writing, to name but a few — wherein they mutually acknowledge each other, albeit in the nearly imperceptible manner of a wink, as Penelope Deutscher rightly puts it (PS, 26). Thinking of both their work,

> one would be hard pressed to distinguish the origin of certain positions. Elliptic greetings, sometimes tense acknowledgments. In one exchange, Derrida and Kofman seem to have been reduced to saying to each other pardon?, pardon?, each supposing that the other is saying to them in rebuke what they take themselves to be saying to the other. (PS, 26–7)

Granted, there are many ways of acknowledging the work of others, and to say that one can cite without citing is hardly news — and I am not speaking about plagiarism, of course.[8] That being said, while references to Derrida are, in Kofman's case, bountiful and usually quite explicit, it is evident that, in Derrida's case, they are more laconic, as if he were attempting to speak to a debt owed once and for all (even as, conversely, it must be reiterated and returned, 'given back' (I, 27) each time, without any final settlement).

Such is the case in *Spurs*, for instance. Deutscher notes that

> Derrida's work *Spurs* is one of the few places where he acknowledges the work of Kofman on Nietzsche, amongst others, readings to which, he says, he owes 'a

great debt (...) that debt itself should (...) be (...) presupposed in its totality'. (*Spurs*, p. 37). (PS, 26)

In fact, the debt acknowledged by Derrida turns out to be even less explicit, as Kofman's name is only one of many 'works' whose so-called authors' names are mentioned in passing, in a footnote and between brackets. The full passage reads as follows: 'I owe these readings a great debt and it is neither through omission nor in a spirit of presumptuous independence that I do not refer to them individually (...) that debt itself should not be fragmented here, but at each moment presupposed in its totality.'[9] Even as it remains consistent with the 'enigmatic operation of the abyssal gift (*le don s'endette/le don sans dette*)' (S, 121) that Derrida analyses in *Spurs*, this gesture is somewhat equivocal, contrary to the iterability of the 'each and every time' that Derrida painstakingly deploys everywhere else in his philosophical work.

Other, more significant Kofman-related omissions are no less surprising. *Aporias* is one such instance: it does not mention *Comment s'en sortir?* at all, even though the latter volume, published in 1983, covers the exact same ground.[10] One encounters the same silence in 'What is a "Relevant" Translation?' with regard to *The Merchant of Venice* and the figure of Shylock.[11] Indeed, Derrida's reading (which touches on forgiveness, a question that lies at the heart of his posthumous tribute to Kofman) rather inexplicably glosses over *Conversions*.[12] This is also the case with 'A Silkworm of One's Own',[13] which picks up his meditation on the veil, hermeneutics and the question of truth where he left off, in *Spurs* and *Glas*. Once again, he does not cite Kofman, even as certain passages from *Lectures de Derrida* could have crossed Derrida's mind, especially in his commentary of Freud's *Femininity* or in his lengthy notes on the curtains of the tabernacle, where he explicitly doubles back on *Glas*. The question of fetishism, which is particularly important, makes up the nodal point of the *différend* between the two philosophers that began at the first Cerisy-la-Salle conference in 1980, 'Les fins de l'homme' (The Ends of Man), where Kofman presented 'Ça cloche'.[14] In this heated debate summed up by Penelope Deutscher,

Derrida takes Kofman to suppose that the fantasy of castration is a master signifier, and responds that this supposes a metaphysical approach to fetishism with an original, master signifier and its substitutes. But Kofman takes herself to be arguing specifically against the idea of castration as a master signifier. (PS, 34n. 28)

This discussion on fetishism reveals itself to be one of the salient points of their correspondence, as evidenced by this passage in which Kofman enthusiastically comments on Derrida's 'Fors', his Foreword to Abraham and Torok's *The Wolf Man's Magic Word*:

> if what lies inside this 'artificial unconscious' is in any case repressed within the 'real unconscious', it is hard to grasp the necessity of making up this whole crypt (...) because it is hard to see how it differs from *hysteria*: you say, they say, here, *jouissance has taken place*; has it really taken place, differently from the way it might for a hysteric, i.e. fantasmatically? Unless I'm mis-reading here, nowhere is there any mention of an original 'rubbing' (*frottement*) on the sister's part that might have taken place? (with him).
>
> I must be misunderstanding something... What do you think? Having a good understanding of this matters to me (...).
>
> Tell me what you make of all this —[15]

Such non-encounter between their respective approaches is again obvious in *The Gift of Death*, as Derrida lengthily analyses the scene of Abraham/Isaac's sacrifice, making no mention of Kofman's interpretation in her 'L'art de ne pas payer ses dettes' (The Art of Not Paying One's Debts).[16] Rereading the seductive figure of Don Juan through Abraham's sacrifice is a rather original premise, to say the least, one that reintroduces the figure of the mother, which an entire tradition had left out. By the same token, Kofman asserts the power of apparently 'irrelevant' details, which became the privileged angle of her reading practice as well as Derrida's:

> In taking up classic texts such as Molière's *Dom Juan*, I always manage to say unusual things by taking specific details as my starting point; this gives my readers an impression of truth. Starting from the next detail — the father saying 'I have long prayed for the heavens to give me a son' — it occurred to me that Dom Juan was born to old parents and I built my entire construction on that.[17]

Among all of 'Sarah's gifts' (I, 1) that he is intent on hailing, Derrida thus 'forgets' the originality of this reading, at once so different from his and perhaps too close to it (Kofman's own interpretation in 'L'art de ne pas payer ses dettes' does indeed intersect with that of 'Counterfeit Money' in *Given Time*).

In short, we are dealing with both gift and counter-gift, both repentance and forgiveness. In his posthumous tribute, Derrida makes much of Sarah's laughter, recalling the biblical scene: laughter upon the announcement of a late pregnancy. He also draws attention to Sarah's name change (which is hardly without resonance in light of her having undergone a forced Christian conversion of her forename, from Sarah to Suzanne, during the Occupation), Sarah being given a nickname by Elohim, as well as the ensuing laughter. Yet it is precisely in this passage that Derrida spells out, in the most striking manner, the aporia of forgiveness, by tying it to this name change:

> The moment having come to laugh was also the moment when Elohim named Sarah. He gave her a new name, deciding that Abraham, who had himself just received another name (changed from Abram to Abraham), would no longer call her Sarai, my princess, but Sarah, princess. So what then? *Comment s'en sortir?* To this question in the form of an aporia, I know of no satisfying answer. Not even crazed laughter. Nothing is given in advance for an act of forgiveness, no rule, no criterion, no norm. It is the chaos at the origin of the world. The abyss of this nonanswer or nonresponse would be the condition of responsibility — decision and forgiveness, the decision to forgive without any concept, if there ever is any. And always (in) the name of the other. (I, 33)

It is interesting to note that, just as Derrida pays special attention in the scene, the scene of reading with which he confronts Sarah Kofman, to the *corpse* over which he watches and the peal of laughter that he wishes to acknowledge until the very end, until the final instant of her death, in a similar way Abraham is described as the one who 'requests a place for her. A final dwelling, a final resting place (. . .) to give her a burial place worthy of her, but also a place that would separate her from him, like death from life' (I, 33). In this way he separates himself from her in the laughter-of-birth insofar as Sarai (my princess), upon becoming Sarah (princess), becomes independent of him (the change in letter, which honours her fecundity, marks a shift in status, both an elevation and a separation). Birth and death are thus closely entwined in the biblical scene no less than in Derrida's scene of reading, which doubles back on it.

Lastly, there is another act of extreme avoidance on Derrida's part that needs to be pointed out. Indeed, how can one *not* note the deafening silence that greets the publication of *Rue Ordener, rue Labat*, the same year as Maurice Blanchot's *The Instant of My Death* (1994), a book that stunned Derrida and to which he dedicated his well-known, painstaking study, *Demeure*?[18] That he should not tease out the proximity between these two works, whether in relation to the question of trauma, of *après coup*, or of witnessing and narrative, seems quite surprising indeed. By contrast, Derrida makes a significant allusion to *Smothered Words* in one of the fragments he wrote in Frédéric Brenner's *Diaspora* (2003), a suite in which he is perhaps at his most defenceless with regard to 'his' Jewish question. In a fragment entitled 'No Freeze Frame', which deals with the gas chambers, his recourse to Kofman's work is nothing less than fascinating:

> Here the gas chamber will have been treated as *technical* apparatus (...), in the intimacy of a *camera obscura*, that machine that da Vinci, along with some other painters, utilized in order to produce an eye without point of view, the illusion of an absolute gaze of God: without perspective. Marx, Nietzsche, and Freud at least took account of the figure of this process of an inverted image in the 'obscure chamber.' My friend Sarah Kofman devoted a book to it: *Camera Obscura: Of Ideology* (...). The rabbi who was her father died at Auschwitz, and in a certain way she will have been unable to survive that. Time to re-read *Smothered Words*.[19]

In this passage that directly pertains to the Shoah, Derrida thus chooses to stress not only his friendship with Sarah Kofman but also the old and unbreakable link that ties him to her work as a reader (*Camera Obscura* is from 1973), unexpectedly likening these two obscure chambers and mentioning, by way of an elliptical shortcut that may seem a bit abrupt, the death of Sarah's father ('The rabbi who was her father', he writes, making use of an odd anteposition) at Auschwitz, as well as her own suicide ('Sarah Kofman took her life in 1994'), thereby endorsing a type of biographical interpretation that he had always viewed with the utmost circumspection.[20]

★

Between Kofman and Derrida, between Derrida and Kofman, the dissymmetry of the relationship is undoubtedly what calls for analysis. A slightly odd, shaky, *unheimlich* scene takes shape here: something seems a little off, 'ça cloche', as one of the two gives too much and takes the expression of her gratitude too far, whereas the other gives too little. Deutscher astutely points out the intersection or chiasmus that is at work here between Derrida and Kofman:

> Kofman seems to engage in an excessive acknowledgement of intellectual debts, her books insistently acknowledging and recognising colleagues who rarely acknowledge her in turn, her books systematically given as (loving?, aggressive?, excruciating?) gifts to the friends whose work she acknowledged. In the face of this, (...) the infrequency of explicit recognition of Kofman in Derrida's work seems the strongest rebuke, as merciless a refusal to play the game of debt, gift, and recognition with her, as was merciless Kofman's relentless insistence on the economy of the debt. (PS, 30)

It is worth pointing out that in this affective scene where sexual difference also has a part to play, 'too much' and 'too little' are not at odds with each other. On the contrary: they bind the relationship together and spur each other on. The stakes on both sides (but more strongly on Kofman's side) would thus be as follows: how to give the other their due; what is more, while becoming '*inde-pendant*' (P, 21 and 46; a recurrent expression in Kofman's work), thus freeing both parties from their obligation?

I obviously shall not go as far as to claim, on the basis of these few examples, that Kofman's works are subject to obliteration on Derrida's part, which would be a most unfair exaggeration, but between the *tribute* he belatedly pays to her *work-life* as a thinker and actual *acknowledgement* in the field (which is something else entirely), one must admit that there is a certain imbalance.[21] In fact, Derrida subscribes to this assessment from the get-go, accusing himself and denouncing what could always turn out to be a mere 'stratagem':

> Some might consider my granting such a privilege to this last text, to the reaffirmation of the work of life as work of art, to be a stratagem on my part, a ruse to conjure away death in my turn, and, through this ruse, which I do not deny, a sort of protestation against her death (. . .). A lesson in protestation. In nonnegative protestation. But also a lesson in the fact that 'protestation' will have been, I now realize as I listen to all the resonances of this word, the privileged mode, the most constant and most common tonality of our face-to-face encounters.
>
> Throughout our entire friendship, (. . .) we protested, sometimes even against one another, right up until the end, and I catch myself still protesting. I catch myself still making a scene before her, as I said earlier, and I smile over this, while smiling to her, as if over a sign of life, in reconciliation. And when it comes to scenes, I have to say that I'll never be able to make as many as she did; I'll never catch up (*Je serai toujours en reste*). (I, 21–2)

This restraint is no doubt a deliberate decision on Derrida's part, who may have been seeking to protect his close friends from the virulent attacks to which he was often exposed. There are undeniable rivalries, tensions, withdrawals and exchanges that will have to be examined in the future, in greater archival depth, while taking into account contexts, shifts and *différances* between Kofman's and Derrida's respective positions on so many of the questions that they share. But this does not explain everything and remains insufficient, '*en reste*', to quote Derrida's meaningful use of this expression, rendered here as 'I'll never catch up'. Without speaking of a gap or *écart*, things are not quite so simple, as they never are with Derrida, and it is important to recall what he himself says about the nature of his relationship with Sarah, and the interminable analysis it calls for:

> These interests (*jeux*) and exercises go so far beyond the limits of a short narrative, indeed of a terminable analysis, that I will not even attempt to speak of them. Those interested will find innumerable small signs in our respective publications. These *remains* are little more than elliptical greetings, sometimes just a wink; they *remain* to be interpreted by anyone, including myself, for I am not always certain from where I stand today that I am still able to decipher them. (I, 3, emphasis mine)

We must attend to these winks and to the nuanced interpretation that these 'perhaps', these inter-dictions, imply. Starting from the wink, from the secret complicity it discreetly signifies, overstepping phenomenological perception and understanding, one could indeed argue that it is the shape *par excellence* of double meaning as conceived by Freud and claimed in turn by Kofman (L, 81).

★

Let us now turn, in closing, to the *pièce de résistance(s)* that is Derrida's magnificent tribute in *Les Cahiers du Grif*. In calling it 'magnificent', I do not only mean to pay tribute to him but also to allow the meaning he etched into this word to resonate further: 'Spectral memory, cinema is a magnificent mourning, a magnified work of mourning.'[22] What is involved here is indeed a *magnified* work of mourning, across both sides of the *Janus bifrons*, the maniacal-melancholic figure so dear to Kofman that goes from tears to laughter, a laughter that causes one's sides to split.[23] This splitting or fragmentation imprints its very shape upon Derrida's piece, in which the two affects are inseparably entwined and where laughter itself is a 'two-faced Janus', as Kofman points out in citing Baudelaire's 'On the Essence of Laughter', a text which causes her to comment that laughter is 'linked to duplicity'.[24]

Derrida gives us a masterclass in reading here, through the *mise en abyme* that lies at the core of his take on 'Conjuring Death', Kofman's own commentary of Rembrandt's painting *The Anatomy Lesson of Doctor Nicolas Tulp*.[25] Derrida's ostensibly rhapsodic piece is in fact carefully arranged, opening with a long prologue followed by three sections (perhaps mimicking Freud's book on *Jokes and Their Relation to the Unconscious*), in which he refers to several of Sarah Kofman's writings, with a special emphasis on *Pourquoi rit-on?* and the posthumously published 'Conjuring Death'. By favouring, as he so often does in these eulogies, the work's extremities, his aim is to transform the whole body into a corpus, even into what he calls *la corpse*, the word that he specifically coins for Sarah in order to countersign the thought of survival in her work, a word that ties the living and the dead, transgressing the line that runs through three languages, French (*corps*), English (corpse) and German (*Körper*):[26]

> I prefer the English word *corpse* here because it incorporates at once the body [*le corps*], the corpus and the cadaver, and because, when read in French, *la corpse* seems to put the body in the feminine and to become an allusion to sexual difference, if not a respect for it.
>
> *Une corpse*: here would be the subject; there would be the object. (I, 19)

This is another way of saying that *la corpse* is neither subject nor object, *and* that it is simultaneously subject and object, traversing all oppositional couplings, lingering in the in-between, in the *interval* (a figureless figure of spacing) and preferably in the feminine (or as the unmarked point of resistance of a thought of the feminine); an *interval* that Derrida marks four times in his text by repeating the expression 'some twenty years apart' (I, 20 and 22). *La corpse*, might one say, is what *remains between*, without substantializing itself or 'being', somewhat like the figure hanging between the two thieves that Sarah Kofman analyses in *Pourquoi rit-on?* This 'missing link' that allows us to 'understand what [discourse] means to say without saying it' (P, 85) is perhaps what instils the shape, through imitation (whether it is conscious or unconscious is beside the point), of Derrida's own reading in his piece.

One could also suggest that this *unheimlich* word — at the point of contact between life and death, which makes up, in this piece where Derrida develops, in the third and most important section, the question of forgiveness in line with the Derridean im-possible — is thus offered 'by way of forgiveness' (I, 26), as the very word through which forgiveness may occur. Derrida's expression, '*en guise de pardon*', is also quite interesting because it is the third and final interpolation he inserts into the Jewish joke of *Pourquoi rit-on?*. These interruptions are striking in that they mimic the conversation picking up where the two friends left it, with Derrida adding that, 'As I said, we must have told this Jewish joke to each other, and probably while eating. And we must have agreed that it was not only funny but memorable, unforgettable, precisely insofar as it treats this treatment of memory called forgiveness' (I, 27). The rejoinders inserted by Derrida ventriloquize and completely alter the joke, breaking the rhythm of the lines, which is essential to their comical effect. In a complex manner, these interpolations themselves double the dialogue between the two Jews in the story even as they also precipitate its ruin, since the final insertion between brackets, '[by way of forgiveness]', flattens the pun and its final punchline. This way of citing or commenting cannot but bring to mind Kofman's own style and her use of generalized grafting, which diverts and transforms the original text. Furthermore, Derrida draws our attention to the simulacrum that can always insinuate itself into forgiveness at the most crucial moment, precisely by diverting the idiomatic '*en guise de*' so as to make the guise or even disguise more apparent.

Above all, we must remember that, for Derrida, 'One only ever asks forgiveness for the unforgivable' (GD, 127). What is at stake is knowing whether, on the one hand, forgiveness can be truly said, can truly take place in literary fiction, as he will ask with reference to Kafka's *Letter to His Father* but also, on the other hand, if forgiveness ever 'really took place, outside of literature' (GD, 145):

> Is forgiveness that is literary or fictive still forgiveness? Unless it were the case that the most effective experience, the concrete endurance of a forgiveness either requested or granted, had (...) its destiny guaranteed in the cryptic gift of the poem, in the body of the literary crypt ... Forgiveness would thus be the poem, the gift of the poem. (GD, 145, translation modified)

Is not something of the sort at play in this piece in which Derrida sets the scene for all of these scenes that he recounts, making a scene, even beyond death, before his friend? Scenes in which he takes pleasure — albeit a pleasure that is inextricably tied to pain, to the suffering of loss — in accusing and excusing himself, in attesting, protesting, disputing and — above all, perhaps — in always thinking, with and thanks to Sarah Kofman, the very test of forgiveness, in the place where it matters, at the very heart of friendship, and of the keenest mourning. Is this not what is at play, before and for us third-party readers and witnesses who confirm the scene as scene? Is this not what is at play particularly in this 'Jewish joke' in which incorrigibly, pitilessly, yet also paradoxically, tenderly, perhaps with an 'infinite compassion for one another, at the very moment (...) when they recognize that they cannot disarm' (I, 30), these two friends laugh in spite of it all, together yet impersonally? Kofman describes such a scene in *Pourquoi rit-on?*: 'laughter doesn't properly belong to anyone, neither in the first nor in the third person. It does not belong to anyone: neither to me nor you, we do not laugh; *people laugh*, together, in an impersonal and neutral manner, through a movement of panic that wrests everyone from their selves' (P, 114). In this Jewish joke, no particular person has the last word, it is only ever *someone* who has the last word. *Pardon pardon*, I'm sorry, I didn't quite catch what you said — but as with Kafka's Abraham, called out from the back of the class by the schoolmaster, it is impossible to ask him to repeat. Is not there forgiveness *there*, in this interstice, perhaps, only ever perhaps, in this wink, this subtle smile, even as the two Jews of the joke, who also stand in for these two friends who undergo the test of forgiveness, in a scene somewhere between simulacrum and reality, act in this way simultaneously, at the keenest point of discord, when forgiveness is an ordeal? This is a forgiveness that stands both in the immemorial time of Jewish history, and on the line that divides 'life death' for the two friends:

> For where is forgiveness more impossible and hence possible in its impossibility, than beyond the boundary dividing the living and the dead? How can a living person ever forgive someone who is dead? What meaning and what gift would there be, in a forgiveness that can no longer hope to reach its destination, except within the self, towards the other welcomed, like a narcissistic ghost within oneself? And conversely, how can a living person hope to be forgiven by someone dead or by a spectre within themselves? (I, 30)

Such is the question that haunts this whole piece as it holds its breath, the breath of life, of survival, of 'life's reprieve' (I, 30) that intensifies the piece in such a singular manner. Does Derrida ask Sarah for forgiveness or not? Does he do so both in truth and through a simulacrum, under the guise of a Jewish joke, and its fictional register? Who could answer this abyssal, impossible question, answer *for* it? And yet, Derrida writes that he 'bet[s] that this insurmountable limit — surmounted, nonetheless, as insurmountable, in the setting free of what is insuperable in the unsurmounted — is indeed the line that our two Jews have crossed, with or within the confession, though without repentance, of their reciprocal accusation' (I, 30).

'So what then?', as Derrida often asks in this piece. What else? What about the reader in this joke about two Jews? Kofman writes in *Pourquoi rit-on?* that 'from the perspective of *Witz*, there is a structural, topical and economic necessity to be understood, conveyed, peddled: without the presence of a third party, indeed, its process *qua* process would be neither achieved nor accomplished' (P, 100). If this is the case, how are we *not* to think about this as we reread the 'Jewish joke' peddled by Kofman, then peddled again by Derrida in his tribute (and by the third-party reader I myself am): a replay, into infinity, of offence and forgiveness, of 'beginning again' and of survival, of *survivance* in action.

La corpse is thus more and something other than a word: it comes to mark, like a poetic sign, the point of reconciliation between the two friends, the point that abolishes all of their differences of opinion, perfect agreement on a given point, a mere point that trumps all others: the question of life, of survival, 'the affirmation of life is nothing other than a certain thought of death; it is neither opposition nor indifference to death — indeed one would almost say the opposite if this were not giving in to opposition' (I, 8).

Of all the acts Derrida thinks and performs in this piece — attesting, pro-testing, peddling, countering, forgiving — this affirmation is no doubt the most important. Of all the things shared by the two philosophers, the question of survival, so bound up with Nietzsche and Blanchot, is that on which they agree the most. One could even say that this point of agreement — this 'yes yes' — prevails over all of their disagreements.

This Derridean piece is thus indeed an 'oblique offering', a gift and a forgiveness where, like in the Jewish joke that gives the 'last word' to laughter, everything can begin again. These pages ought to be carefully reread, '*Let read* (...) *let* (...) *live*', as Derrida encouraged us to. In other words, this Derridean reconfiguration of the concept of forgiveness does owe — a debt without debt yet not without gratitude — something to Sarah Kofman, and maybe more than could ever be said, let alone repaid.

(Translated by COSMIN TOMA)

NOTES

1 Sarah Kofman, *Pourquoi rit-on? Freud et le mot d'esprit* (Paris: Galilée, 1986), 198, hereafter P. This is the book's very last paragraph. Derrida discusses it at length in his untitled tribute to Sarah Kofman in *Les Cahiers du Grif* 3:1 (1997), 131–66; translated by Pascale-Anne Brault and Michael Naas as 'Introduction' in Sarah Kofman, *Selected Writings*, edited by Thomas Albrecht, with Georgia Albert and Elizabeth Rottenberg (Stanford, CA: Stanford University Press, 2007), 1–34, hereafter I. Interestingly, Derrida commented on this very same passage in the fifth session of his 1996–1997 EHESS seminar 'Hostilité/hospitalité'. A significant portion of it was reused a few months later, in April 1997, for his tribute to Sarah Kofman in *Les Cahiers du Grif.* The session was translated into English by Gil Anidjar, in *Jacques Derrida: Acts of Religion*, edited and with an introduction by Anidjar (New York and

London: Routledge, 2002), 356–420. (Translator's note: The first paragraph of the above quotation is from Kofman, *Selected Writings*, 26; the final sentence is my translation. Unless otherwise indicated, all translations are my own.)

2 Sarah Kofman, *Lectures de Derrida* (Paris: Éditions Galilée, 1984), hereafter L; Sarah Kofman, 'Un philosophe "unheimlich"' in *Écarts: Quatre essais à propos de Jacques Derrida*, with Lucette Finas, Roger Laporte and Jean-Michel Rey (Paris: Fayard, 1973), 107–204; reprinted in *Lectures de Derrida*; Sarah Kofman, 'Ça cloche', translated by Caren Kaplan, in *Continental Philosophy II: Derrida and Deconstruction*, edited by Hugh J. Silverman (New York and London: Routledge, 1989), 108–38. See also Sarah Kofman, 'Ça cloche', translated by Thomas Albrecht, in *Selected Writings*, 71–95, and Jacques Derrida, *Glas*, translated by John P. Leavey Jr. and Richard Rand (Lincoln, NE and London: University of Nebraska Press, 1986).

3 Penelope Deutscher, 'Pardon: Sarah Kofman and Jacques Derrida (On Mourning, Debts and Seven Friendships)', *Journal of the British Society of Phenomenology* 31:1 (2000), 27–8, http://dx.doi.org/10.1080/00071773.2000.11007277, hereafter PS.

4 Here, Kofman cites Jacques Derrida's 'The Double Session' in *Dissemination* (London and New York: Continuum, 2004 [1981]), 203.

5 Sarah Kofman, '*Subvertir le philosophique* ou *Pour un supplément de jouissance*' [interview with Evelyne Ender], *Compar(a)ison* 1 (1993), 9–26 (23).

6 Sylviane Agacinski, Jacques Derrida, Sarah Kofman, Philippe Lacoue-Labarthe, Jean-Luc Nancy and Bernard Pautrat, *Mimesis des articulations* (Paris: Aubier-Flammarion, 1975).

7 Sarah Kofman, 'Lettre à Jacques Derrida, le 30 octobre 1975' in Ginette Michaud and Isabelle Ullern, *Sarah Kofman et Jacques Derrida: croisements, écarts, différences* (Paris: Hermann, 2018), 188–9.

8 Kofman is very sensitive to this, noting that the word 'plagiarism' is tied to a citational reading–writing practice that parodies 'the citationality of all writing and the absence of paternity'. Sarah Kofman, 'No Longer Full-Fledged *Autobiogriffies*', translated by Winnie Woodhull, *SubStance* 29 (1981), 3–22 (16).

9 Jacques Derrida, *Spurs: Nietzsche's Styles/Éperons. Les styles de Nietzsche*, translated by Barbara Harlow (Chicago: University of Chicago Press, 1979), 37, hereafter S.

10 Jacques Derrida, *Aporias*, translated by Thomas Dutoit (Stanford, CA: Stanford University Press, 1993); Sarah Kofman, *Comment s'en sortir?* (Paris: Galilée, 1983). For partial translations of *Comment s'en sortir?*, see also Sarah Kofman, 'Nightmare. At the Margins of Medieval Studies', translated by Frances Bartkowski, in *Selected Writings*, 251–4, and 'Beyond Aporia?', translated by David Macey, in *Post-structuralist Classics*, edited by Andrew Benjamin (London and New York: Routledge, 1988), 7–44.

11 Jacques Derrida, 'What is a "Relevant" Translation?', translated by Lawrence Venuti, *Critical Inquiry* 27:2 (2001), 174–200.

12 Sarah Kofman, 'Conversions: *The Merchant of Venice* under the Sign of Saturn', translated by Shaun Whiteside, in *Literary Theory Today*, edited by Peter Collier and Helga Geyer-Ryan (Cambridge: Polity Press, 1990), 142–66.

13 Jacques Derrida, 'A Silkworm of One's Own (Points of View Stitched on the Other Veil)', translated by Geoffrey Bennington, *Oxford Literary Review* 18:1/2 (1996), 3–65. Is it because he lengthily quotes Cixous on Freud's *Femininity* that *The Enigma of Woman* does not cross his mind?

14 See Kofman, 'Ça cloche'. In the *Cahiers du Grif*'s 'bibliography', the following is specified: 'continuous comments by S. K.: p. 16, 47, 86–87, 184, 196, 199, 310, 341, 365, 391–392, 410, 497, 650–1)'. Reprinted (without the discussion but with additional notes) in *Lectures de Derrida*, 115–51. This attention to detail is indeed the mark of a true debate.

15 See Sarah Kofman, 'Lettre à Jacques Derrida, le 6 août 1976' in Michaud and Ullern, *Sarah Kofman et Jacques Derrida*, 200–2.

16 Jacques Derrida, *The Gift of Death*, second edition, and *Literature in Secret*, translated by David Wills (Chicago and London: University of Chicago Press), 2008, hereafter GD.

17 Kofman, '*Subvertir le philosophique* ou *Pour un supplément de jouissance*', 23.

18 Maurice Blanchot, *The Instant of My Death*/Jacques Derrida, *Demeure: Fiction and Testimony*, translated by Elizabeth Rottenberg (Stanford, CA: Stanford University Press, 2000).

19 Jacques Derrida, 'No Freeze Frame', translated by Peggy Kamuf, in Frédéric Brenner, *Diaspora: Homelands in Exile, Vol. 2: Voices* (New York: HarperCollins, 2003), 83, translation modified. Derrida also quotes, in a footnote, two passages from *Smothered Words*, translated by Madeleine Dobie (Evanston, IL: Northwestern University Press, 1998), 7 and 9: one about 'Auschwitz, 'a name beyond naming', and the other underscoring the aporia of witnessing in *Smothered Words*: 'How can it not be said? And how can it be said? How can one speak of that before which all possibility of speech ceases?' The note ends on this sentence, which stresses suicide: 'Sarah Kofman took her life in 1994.'

20 Sarah Kofman, *Camera Obscura: Of Ideology*, translated by Will Straw (Ithaca, NY: Cornell University Press, 1999). Jacques Derrida also quotes this volume regarding the 'general question of fetishization' in *Specters of Marx: The State of the Debt, the Work of Mourning and the New International*, translated by Peggy Kamuf, with an introduction by Bernd Magnus and Stephen Cullenberg (New York and London: Routledge, 2006), 209.

21 See, for instance, Jacques Derrida, *Memoirs of the Blind: The Self-Portrait and Other Ruins*, translated by Pascale-Anne Brault and Michael Naas (Chicago and London: University of Chicago Press, 1993), 63n. 59. On the subject

of castration anxiety as it relates to the fear of losing one's eyes, Derrida refers to Kofman's interpretation in 'The Double is/and the Devil' in *Freud and Fiction*, translated by Sarah Wykes (Boston, MA: Northeastern University Press; Cambridge: Polity Press, 1991), 119–62.

22 Jacques Derrida, 'Cinema and Its Ghosts: An Interview with Jacques Derrida', translated by Peggy Kamuf, *Discourse: Journal for Theoretical Studies in Media and Culture* 37:1–2 (2015), 28.

23 See, among other texts, Sarah Kofman, *Pourquoi rit-on?*, 74f., and *Socrates: Fictions of a Philosopher*, translated by Catherine Porter (London: Athlone Press, 1998).

24 Charles Baudelaire, 'On the Essence of Laughter' in *Selected Writings on Art & Artists*, translated by P. E. Charvet (Cambridge: Cambridge University Press, 1972), 148; cited by Sarah Kofman in *Pourquoi rit-on?*, 75n. 17. On this laughter, see also Sarah Kofman, 'Un battu imbattable' and 'Angoisse et catharsis' in *L'Imposture de la beauté et autres textes* (Paris: Galilée, 1995), 131–7 and 141–5.

25 See Sarah Kofman, 'Conjuring Death: Remarks on *The Anatomy Lesson of Doctor Nicolas Tulp* (1632)', translated by Pascale-Anne Brault, in *Selected Writings*, 237–41 (238). On this article, see Pleshette DeArmitt's remarkable analysis, 'Conjuring Bodies: Kofman's Lesson on Death', *Parallax* 17:1 (2011), 4–17, as well as my essay '"Traiter de l'intraitable". Remarques sur la pensée de l'esthétique de Sarah Kofman dans *Mélancolie de l'art*' in *Penser en commun? Un 'rapport sans rapport'*, edited by Isabelle Ullern and Pierre Gisel (Paris: Beauchesne, 2015), 201–33.

26 Is this transformation a reminiscence of the Jewish rite whereby one must, at the moment of burying the body in a shroud (the *tallit* for men), gather the body in its entirety, all of its *membra disjecta*? As is well known, this figure haunts the conception of the body (*corps-corpus*) in all of Kofman's philosophical work.

Derrida's Missing Woman

CHARLOTTE THEVENET

> I too am a child and I love to laugh and love to be loved. I have been touched by many things in your text, even though I am not your 'destined one [destinée]', not even ever directly destined, never 'named' like so many others.[1]
>
> Sarah Kofman, Letter to Jacques Derrida, 8 October 1979

As many critics have noted, while Kofman refers abundantly to Derrida, 'Sarah Kofman' as a corpus and as a proper name is not as visible in Derrida's work as one could expect. Ginette Michaud, in the book she recently published with Isabelle Ullern, looks back on this odd dissymmetry. Commenting on 'several manifest absences on Derrida's part, who does not acknowledge Kofman's work as often as one could have expected', she points to many of the questions the two philosophers have in common: 'woman, babelism and translation, representation and imitation, metaphor, autobiographical writing'.[2] Michaud lists several examples of Derrida's curious silences regarding Kofman's work: *Aporias* does not refer to *Comment s'en sortir?* ('Beyond Aporia?'), 'What is a "Relevant" Translation?' does not cite *Conversions: The Merchant of Venice under the Sign of Saturn* and 'A Silkworm of One's Own', which comments on Freud's lecture on *Femininity*, does not acknowledge Kofman's extensive commentary on it in *The Enigma of Woman,* nor does he refer to Kofman's analyses of his own work in *Lectures de Derrida* (Readings of Derrida).[3]

Reading this inventory, one gets the feeling that Derrida and Kofman share the very matter of their writing, its *inventio*; does Derrida not intimate, in the eulogy he wrote for Kofman, paraphrasing her own intimation in 'The Melancholy of Art', that 'it is necessary "to invent"', thus perhaps obliquely acknowledging his friend's talent for invention?[4] It is understood that any recognition of debt on Derrida's

Paragraph 44.1 (2021): 58–72
DOI: 10.3366/para.2021.0354

www.euppublishing.com/para

part remains oblique at best. However, as Penelope Deutscher explains, there is a stark contrast between the way the two thinkers engage with one another. On the one hand, Kofman regularly addresses her counterpart 'in an excessive acknowledgment of intellectual debt, her books insistently acknowledging and recognizing colleagues who rarely acknowledge her in turn'; on the other, there is an 'infrequency of explicit recognition of Kofman in Derrida's work' which can appear as 'the strongest rebuke, as merciless a refusal to play the game of debt, gift, and recognition with her, as was merciless Kofman's relentless insistence on the economy of the debt'.[5] Although Deutscher shows that ultimately there is more than a flat refusal in Derrida's silence — 'the understanding that there can be no understanding between us in the proximity of our impossibility' (P, 32) — one cannot but wonder at Derrida's erasure of Kofman's proper name. It is particularly visible — perhaps even too visible to be a naïve erasure — in the text he wrote as her eulogy: the blank space that is its title contrasts with titles that instead put forward, play with, or simply mention a friend's proper name: *Signéponge/Signsponge*, *H. C. For Life, That Is to Say . . .*, *Demeure: Maurice Blanchot*, *On Touching: Jean-Luc Nancy*, *Shibboleth: For Paul Celan*, *Memoires: For Paul de Man*.[6]

I thus consider that 'Sarah Kofman', as a cited corpus, and as a readable, decipherable proper name, is missing from Derrida's texts. I propose to read and articulate this absence with another erasure discernible in Derrida's corpus, the erasure of 'woman'.[7] My bringing together of 'Sarah Kofman' and 'woman' rests on two observations: first, that of a formal analogy between 'Sarah Kofman' and 'woman' in Derrida's texts as they are both present and erased from them. One could hardly argue that 'woman' is absent from Derrida's corpus, just as we have seen that Sarah Kofman's work is very much present in her friend's texts; but although both are present thematically, both end up being erased: Kofman's name hardly ever appears in Derrida's work, her thinking, though present, does not get the acknowledgement one would expect, just as 'woman' also finally goes missing. Moreover, the common erasure of 'woman' and 'Sarah Kofman' is concerning if one recalls that Spivak problematizes the question of woman in Derrida's work as that of the '(non)name of woman'.[8] Second, 'Sarah Kofman' has everything to do with 'woman'. The corpus called 'Sarah Kofman' is, in its vast majority, dedicated to the history of the category of 'woman' in philosophy, and more broadly stems from a constant preoccupation with the function of the feminine in the texts it comments on.[9] What if 'Sarah Kofman' was the name of

Derrida's missing 'woman'? What if the erasure of 'Sarah Kofman' in Derrida's corpus had to do with the erasure of 'woman' in those same texts? I shall explore this possibility through a threefold argument: first, drawing on feminist writings from the 1980s, I shall argue that Derrida's instrumental use of 'woman' leads to an erasure. Then, I shall show that even when Derrida actually addresses 'woman', the reference to 'woman' functions at the level of style, never at the level of *ethos* nor of reference.[10] Finally, I shall focus on Derrida's commentary on Kofman's late text to show how missing women and the philosophers' own positions regarding gender are at play in both of the texts in question.

Missing: 'Woman'

Before Sarah Kofman was anywhere *not* to be found in Derrida's work, the paradoxical absence of 'woman' was deemed worthy of scrutiny by a range of feminist critics. I propose to reopen an old case in the history of 'French Theory', a case mainly disputed by and between feminist critics mostly in the 1980s.[11] It incriminates French thinkers who, in their endeavour to 'think new relationships' between old categories such as *technē* and *physis*, time and space, man and woman, and so on, used 'woman' and 'the feminine' as the token of something left unexplored until then. Alice Jardine identifies a process of 'transformation of woman and the feminine into verbs' in the postmodern narratives that she calls gynesis.[12] As she puts it — and other feminist critics observed the same trend — 'it has become increasingly difficult to find a major theoretician in France today [1985] who is not concerned in one way or another with "woman", the "feminine", or variations thereof. (...) The "feminine" has become (...) "a metaphor without brakes"' (GC, 34).[13] Derrida is no exception. The hypothesis I would like to pursue here draws on the work of Jardine and Spivak, but also that of Miller, Schor and Collin, Michaud and Berger, and questions Derrida's use of words related to a woman's body in order to coin his undecidables (for example, 'hymen', '*erion*' or fleece, 'invagination'). I argue that Derrida's putting into discourse of 'woman' is fetishistic inasmuch as the coining of undecidables demands the erasure of 'woman' as generator of undecidables.

One of Derrida's famous moves to renew philosophical writing consists in defining writing as a feminine technique: 'the text is the golden fleece', he writes in *Clang*, before continuing and clarifying the metaphor:[14]

> Writing remains modest [*pudique*] because it is caught in a fleece. Concerning modesty, 'plaiting', 'weaving', and 'matting', Freud applies a natural model to the feminine technique of the text: the hair that hides the genitals and especially, for the woman, the lack of a penis.[15]

Here, Derrida is quoting Freud's lecture on *Femininity*. It all started with 'shame, which is considered to be a feminine characteristic *par excellence* but is far more a matter of convention than might be supposed'; shame is endowed with the role of hiding the defect of female genitalia. While Freud remarks that few inventions were made by women, he concedes that 'there is, however, one technique which they may have invented — that of plaiting and weaving', before immediately correcting himself: 'Nature herself would seem to have given the model which this achievement imitates by causing the growth at maturity of the pubic hair that conceals the genitals'; in other words, all women had to do was to weave the hairs together.[16]

There is a 'feminine technique of the text', both in Freud's and in Derrida's work, but, as Kofman herself did not fail to point out in her commentary on Freud's conference, the attribution of this invention to women is 'at the very least ambiguous' (EW, 49). The paradox is that when women finally seem to be given some credit, they are in fact deprived of their status as inventors. As Kofman explains, 'Freud asserts that modesty, or "shame", is both a *conventional* virtue (more or less linked to cultural repression) and a *natural* one, since, in her invention of weaving, woman was only "imitating" nature' (EW, 49). What merit is there in inventing something that already had a natural model? But that is not all: women's invention strongly depends on the fulfilment of their biological destiny. First, only the lack of a penis gave women the momentum needed to invent weaving. Second, this invention, allowing them to hide what Kofman ironically calls 'that gaping wound that threatens to contaminate [men] (. . .) who would then be condemned to homosexuality' (EW, 49), conditions the survival of the human race; as long as men ignore women's castration, they are able to be aroused by them and thus to engage in reproductive sex. Women were then both taught by nature and *meant* by nature to invent weaving; nature gave them the idea but also pushed them towards weaving by depriving them of a penis and giving them an instinct to reproduce in the first place. In the end, women did not invent anything and only fulfilled their own biological destiny.

When Derrida mentions this 'feminine technique of the text' then, we can wonder whether the adjective refers to an active or to a passive role: is the technique feminine because women invented it, or just because it was invented by nature through the weaving of feminine body hair? The phrase as well as the metaphor of the text as textile, usually used to insist on the process of textuality rather than on the intentionality of its producer, both seem to suggest that the technique is endowed with a degree of femininity that has nothing to do with a female operator.[17] In 'The Double Session', Derrida develops the quasi-concept of 'hymen' that allows him to coin an undecidable logic; that is where we first propose to trace the erasure of 'woman' identified in the feminine technique of the text. The 'hymen' relates to 'woman' in quite a straightforward way: hymen relates to 'woman' because it designates a part of 'woman', the membrane at the entrance of the vagina that is allegedly pierced by the first penetrating intercourse. Derrida borrows the term from Mallarmé who uses it in 'Mimique':

> The scene illustrates but the idea, not any actual action, in a hymen (out of which flows Dream), tainted with vice yet sacred, between desire and fulfilment, perpetration and remembrance: here anticipating, there recalling, in the future, in the past, *under the false appearance of a present*. That is how the Mime operates, whose act is confined to a perpetual allusion without breaking the ice or the mirror: he thus sets ups a medium, a pure medium, of fiction.[18]

The hymen stands on a thin, paradoxical line between unfulfilled desire and accomplished penetrating sexual intercourse. Hymen in fact signifies two contradictory gestures: as marriage, it means the physical union of two bodies, their fusion into one entity, but as a membrane, it points towards the separation of two spaces — the vulva and the vagina — and thus evokes a border, a limit, if not an interdiction. What interests Derrida is precisely the undecidability between the hymen's two contradictory meanings:

> 'Hymen' (...) is first of all a sign of fusion, the consummation of a marriage, the identification of two beings, the confusion between the two. *Between* the two, there is no longer difference but identity. (...) there is no longer any difference between desire and satisfaction. (DS, 209)

This difference without any decidable poles, which is no longer operative, is understood by Derrida in terms of a syntax: 'What counts here is the formal or syntactical *praxis* that builds it up and breaks it down [the word "hymen"]' (DS, 220, translation modified).

At this point in his commentary, Derrida transforms the hymen into something syntactic, a disposition, negotiation, betweenness, an *entre*, even suggesting that the former is dispensable, arguing that 'the hymen must be determined through the *entre* and not the other way around' (DS, 220). I shall contend that Derrida does not: by preferring the grammatical homophone *entre* — it can be a preposition, a verb or a noun — to the noun *hymen*, he privileges a term irreducible to any reference to a word that could actually refer to 'woman', thus erasing the term's very condition of possibility.

Derrida's Use of 'Woman'

One could argue that I have been somehow dishonestly cutting through Derrida's works in order to make my point, and purposely avoiding texts where Derrida addresses 'woman' at greater length than in the passages of *Clang* and 'The Double Session' commented on above. One cannot claim to address the so-called question of woman in Derrida's work without addressing *Spurs*, for example, where the philosopher famously announces: 'The title for this lecture was to have been the question of style. However — it is woman who will be my subject. Still, one might wonder whether that doesn't really amount to the same thing.'[19] Once again, we find the 'question of style' and the question of woman addressed jointly in one text. But, as the use of 'However' followed by the em dash suggests, 'style' and 'woman' do not go harmoniously together; 'however' seems to point to some kind of disjunction and certainly underlines the difficult articulation of 'style' and 'woman'. In one of the last sections of the text, Derrida will come back to his first words and declare: 'so woman, then, will not have been my subject', not because 'woman' has simply been erased in favour of 'style', but because 'there is no such thing (. . .) as a Being or an essence of *the* woman or the sexual difference' (S, 121). What I have called the effacement of 'woman' and its relationship to writing cannot be considered as a negative process; it is rather a deeply ambivalent gesture that certainly permits the deconstruction of the ontological category of 'woman', and thus its de-essentialization.[20]

If 'woman' relates to 'style', it does not relate to any style. 'Woman', always represented laughing, relates to a kind of non-serious, even witty writing that only she seems able to generate. *Clang* resounds with a feminine laughter: that of Antigone, staged laughing at the dialectical process even on the verge of her death: 'Two brothers, standing up to each other, can only kill each other. *Qua* brothers. Which is the death of Antigone, not without her laughing about it as she is the last one to leave' (C, 198a). Antigone figures as yet another trope in the series of Derridean women who die laughing, a series inaugurated by Colombine in 'The Double Session'.

In this text, Derrida mentions at length the different versions of 'The story of Pierrot who tickled his wife, / And thus made her laughingly give up her life', as Gautier would have it (DS, 203).[21] But Colombine does not stop at dying from laughter; once dead, she comes back to haunt her murderer with her laughter:

> [Pierrot] is overtaken, incoercibly, by 'Columbine's tickle, like a contagious, avenging ill'. He tries to escape it by what he calls a 'remedy': the bottle with which another erotic scene concludes in a 'spasm' and a 'swoon'. After the second lapse, a hallucination presents him with a Columbine who has become animate in her portrait, bursting out in laughter. Pierrot is again overcome by trepidation and tickling, and finally he dies at the feet of his 'painted victim laughing still'. (DS, 201–2)

Whilst Pierrot is tickled to death, just like Colombine, he does not laugh; while he is 'again overcome by trepidation and tickling', she looks at him, still laughing.

Why do women laugh, if I may paraphrase one of Kofman's titles?[22] Another scene in *Clang* gives us a clue. It quotes heavily from Genet's *Screens*, where Leïla takes out from under her skirt an incongruous series of objects — 'bits of broken glass ... or fragments ... pieces of glass ... shards ... splinters' — until staging the birth of her 'latest little one', a fake Galalith alarm clock the existence of which is only materialized through a drawing on a screen placed on stage (C, 139b). During the entire scene, Leïla and The Mother are staged laughing. They laugh, first and foremost, at Leïla's performance of simulating birth. But the scene does not only stage a fake delivery, it stages the fake delivery of a fake alarm clock, which at first exists only via a periphrasis, 'my latest little one', then via a drawing. In addition, the fake alarm clock is made of Galalith. Derrida observes: 'All this galactic matter signals fake, not only because its substance is synthetic, but because this cheap bazaar object is merely drawn, and then in *trompe-l'œil*, and on a screen. Interminable funeral [*obsèque*] of the thing itself' (C, 140b). 'Woman' in Derrida appears as the provider of *toc* — whereby resound the fake, but also the *tocsin*, the alarm bell, as well as the tick-tock of the (fake) clock — laughing, she gives (fake) birth to an interminable series of simulacra — 'interminable obsequy of the thing itself'.[23]

'Woman' is then the name of an alternative relationship to Truth, which Derrida himself adopts as writing. At the beginning of 'The Double Session', at the end of a long, polemical, defensive footnote, where Derrida has reminded his readers what he means by 'writing', he evokes one particular misreading of his work, consisting in 'turn[ing] [an old word and an old concept of writing]' against his critique of logocentrism. In order to demonstrate the stupidity of these reactions, Derrida appeals to an example:

> Freud recounts that when he was having trouble gaining acceptance for the possibility of masculine hysteria, he encountered, among these primary sorts of resistance which do not reveal mere foolishness or lack of culture, the resistance of a surgeon who *expressly* told him: 'But, my dear colleague, how can you pronounce such absurdities? *Hysteron* (*sic*) signifies *uterus*. How then can a man be hysterical?' (DS, 182)

Derrida significantly adds: 'The example is not insignificant', as if hinting at an understanding of writing in relation to gender. Finally, the footnote's conclusion seems to confirm that 'woman' and all 'womanly' things can only be second-hand:

> This note, this reference, the choice of this example are placed here merely to herald a certain *out-of-placeness* [*déplacé*] of language: we are thus introduced into what is *supposed* to be found *behind* the hymen: the *hystera* (υστερυ), which exposes itself only by transference and simulacrum—by mimicry. (DS, 182, Derrida's emphasis)

Not only do we hold the clue to the derivativeness of 'woman' — 'the *hystera* (υστερυ), which exposes itself only by transference and simulacrum' — but the lack of origin that appears characteristic of 'woman' goes hand in hand with a stylistic process: 'a certain *out-of-placeness* of language'.

Derrida does not so much address 'woman' in his work as he uses 'woman' to craft his own writing: a writing that is improper (*impropre*), witty, parodic, that functions through syntactical series rather than by referring back to an origin outside the text, and that deconstructs any assumption of essence (as the example of the '*hysteron* (*sic*)' demonstrates). In the light of this I propose to track missing women in both Kofman's essay 'Conjuring Death' and Derrida's commentary upon it.

'Sarah Kofman': Derrida's Woman?

Turning now to Derrida's eulogy for Kofman, we stumble upon an unexpected configuration regarding 'woman', 'women' and more generally regarding the authors' gendered positions. First, Derrida appears to endow Kofman with the same features we highlighted in his work as feminine. The terms in which he presents his hypothesis on Kofman are telling: 'She would cry *for laughs* — that is my thesis or my hypothesis' (I, 7). From laughter to simulacrum, Derrida, by summing up his friend through the phrase *pour rire*, attributes to her the very features he attributes to 'woman' in his texts. The phrase encapsulates the very function of femininity in Derrida's work: women laugh, and women fake.[24]

Looking more carefully at Derrida's commentary, we have to acknowledge that its sexual politics are more complex than just reducing Kofman to a typical Derridean woman, and who would be surprised as, after all, his and Kofman's texts revolve around a corpse, an almost entirely naked one in Kofman's case? Derrida's text first follows Kofman's and points to the 'spiriting away of the proper body' (I, 2) in Rembrandt's *Anatomy Lesson*: the painting, Kofman explains, does not picture a triumph of death but 'a triumph over death', the book of science attracting the gaze and full attention of the men gathered around the corpse.[25] Naming 'la corpse' the dead body at stake in Kofman's text and Rembrandt's *Anatomy Lesson*, thus using the feminine of the French determiner *la* coupled with an *-e* ending, Derrida encompasses 'the body and the cadaver' (I, 9) and introduces sexual difference where Rembrandt's painting erases it. Not only is the cadaver's waist covered with a white cloth, but the oblivion of the flesh at work does not leave any room for sexual difference. 'La corpse' allows Derrida to counterbalance Rembrandt's masculine narrative with a feminine element, at the same time honouring the memory of his female friend Sarah Kofman. But let us note that he does so by maintaining a certain undecidability regarding sexual difference: 'la corpse' is not decisively feminine, and that is precisely what interests Derrida. Although he could be seen as following Kofman here, I shall argue that his move in fact differs from Kofman's.

Curiously, Kofman's text does not seem preoccupied at all by the sexual politics of Rembrandt's painting. The philosopher does not offer a female reverse angle to Rembrandt's masculine triumph over death. In fact, she does little more than mention a possible counterpoint to Rembrandt's anatomy: 'I would thus oppose to this first *Anatomy Lesson* by Rembrandt not, as is normally done, the second one, but rather a painting by Goya, either the *Witches' Sabbath* or the *Pilgrimage of Saint Isidore*' (CD, 240). Kofman offers few explanations for her choice, only writing that

> In those disquieting gatherings, everyone forms a single body through a certain quality of their gazes, oriented this time, however, not by an extreme interest in science but by a common horror and terror. Their eyes are turned not toward some present object, like the cadaver in Rembrandt's painting, but toward something absent, threatening, and unnameable. (CD, 240)

Again, apparently, and for once, sexual difference seems to be kept at bay; Rembrandt and Goya are opposed because of the sentiment expressed in the eyes of their subjects, not because of the sexual politics of their paintings. However, looking at the two paintings cited by Kofman, one could see sexual difference re-emerge, if only because these paintings stage women figures. It is particularly striking in the *Witches' Sabbath*, which shows women of all ages, sometimes holding small children or babies, gathered around a standing goat during a moonlit night. The *Pilgrimage to Saint Isidore* shows women and men walking in a procession. The colour black dominates and the faces are blurry; but the costumes, and particularly the black or white veils covering the women's heads, allow the viewer to distinguish them from the men. I propose to see in these female figures another motif of counterpoint between Goya and Rembrandt. Could we go as far as to argue that Kofman did not choose these paintings randomly and favoured them because they staged women figures when Rembrandt's painting was utterly devoid of any? When Derrida, reading Kofman reading Rembrandt, reintroduces sexual difference through an undecidable neologism that both exhibits the feminine and erases 'woman' — 'la corpse' — Kofman reintroduces 'women' rather than sexual difference into her text, but without saying it, without drawing attention to it, simply mentioning two paintings of another male painter.

Derrida, like Kofman, ends his text with a reference to Blanchot. His is in an endnote that complements the following question asked by Derrida in the last pages of his homage: '*Comment s'en sortir?*' (I, 33). The note reminds the reader of the quote from Blanchot's *The Madness of the Day* that opens and closes Kofman's text. It talks about how men and women deal with mortality, and particularly with a certain triumph of life or triumph over death:

> Men want to escape death, strange beings that they are. And some of them cry out 'Die, die' because they want to escape from life. 'What a life. I'll kill myself. I'll give in.' This is lamentable and strange; it is a mistake. Yet I have met people who have never said to life, 'Quiet!', who have never said to death, 'Go away!' Almost always women, beautiful creatures. (I, 258n. 2)[26]

In other words, men cannot deal with either life or death; mostly, if not only, women know how to try not to triumph over life nor over death. Ironically, in these texts, it is Derrida who exhibits the sexual politics at work in Kofman's commentary on Rembrandt. It is he who shows, through the endnote that closes his text and that echoes Kofman's own ending with a quote from Blanchot, that the reverse angle she opposes to Rembrandt's *Anatomy Lesson* is a woman's lesson.

To conclude, I would like to link this odd complementarity between Derrida's and Kofman's texts — whereby she is the one who seems to persist in an otherwise all-male narrative, and he exhibits her own reintroduction of women into a masculine context while himself erasing 'woman' in favour of the feminine — to the oddly symmetrical positions they have taken regarding their own writing practice and gender.

As feminist critics have noted, Derrida adopted a feminine position of sorts regarding writing. This position — which has more to do with gender than with sexuality — often takes the form of a polygendered discourse, 'a choreographic text with polysexual signatures' that would not pretend to achieve an impossible gender neutrality (whether phallocentric or gynocentric).[27] This is the case in texts such as *Cinders*, which explicitly intertwines feminine and masculine voices.[28] But Derrida went further and claimed to occupy a feminine position; in *The Post Card*, for example, the writer claims that his female lover, his 'very sweet destiny', and he 'are of the same sex'.[29] Catherine Malabou recalls in 'Woman's Possibility, Philosophy's Impossibility' that Derrida used to open his sentences half-jokingly with 'I, as a woman ...', and describes the impossible situation she found herself in as a woman philosopher doing deconstruction in the wake of a male philosopher mimicking femininity.[30] Unlike Malabou, Kofman never wrote on what it was like, for her, to be a woman philosopher, and particularly a woman philosopher close to Derrida. Although received as a *woman* philosopher, especially by the American women critics of the 1980s, and often questioned on her own position in a very masculine field (philosophy, the university), she always rejected the idea of a feminine writing for herself: 'I will never call my writing *feminine*, because speaking of feminine writing means going back to attributing something proper to man, something proper to woman.'[31] She even goes as far as to refuse to say that she writes 'as a woman'; when questioned by Jardine and Menke, she responds: 'One starts from the fact that, apparently, I am (. . .) a woman, and therefore that I write as a woman. In fact, I write as a "philosopher" first and foremost' (SS, 105). While she acknowledges that no discourse is ever devoid of gender or sexuality (and reminds us that she demonstrated as much in her book on Comte), she refuses to see her position as an author labelled 'feminine', arguing that 'the author's position is not to be identified with his or her anatomical sex' (SS, 105). What is striking in the duo formed by Kofman and Derrida may be less the odd dissymmetry of their references to each other — too many on one side, not enough on the other — than the unexpected symmetry of their sexual politics, whereby each of them would explicitly refuse to see their writing assigned to their gender, all the while writing, in persistent ways, as a woman or a man philosopher respectively.

NOTES

1 Letter from Sarah Kofman to Jacques Derrida in Ginette Michaud and Isabelle Ullern, *Sarah Kofman et Jacques Derrida: croisements, écarts, différences* (Paris: Hermann, 2018), 251–52. Unless otherwise indicated, all translations are my own. The date given by Kofman is 8 October 1979, but the true date seems to be 1 October.

2 Ginette Michaud, 'Jacques Derrida lecteur de Sarah Kofman' in Michaud and Ullern, *Sarah Kofman et Jacques Derrida*, 29.

3 Jacques Derrida, *Aporias*, translated by Thomas Dutoit (Stanford, CA: Stanford University Press, 1993); Sarah Kofman, *Comment s'en sortir?* (Paris: Galilée, 1983) (Editor's note: an excerpt of this text is available in translation as 'Beyond Aporia?', translated by David Macey, in *Post-structuralist Classics*, edited by Andrew Benjamin (London and New York: Routledge, 1988), 7–44); Jacques Derrida, 'What is a "Relevant" Translation?", translated by Lawrence Venuti, *Critical Inquiry* 27:2 (2001), 174–200; Sarah Kofman, *Conversions: 'Le Marchand de Venise' sous le signe de Saturne* (Paris: Galilée, 1987); Jacques Derrida, 'A Silkworm of One's Own (Points of View Stitched on the Other Veil)', translated by Geoffrey Bennington, *Oxford Literary Review* 18:1/2 (1996), 3–65; Sarah Kofman, *The Enigma of Woman: Woman in Freud's Writings*, translated by Catherine Porter (Ithaca, NY: Cornell University

Press, 1985), hereafter EW; Sarah Kofman, *Lectures de Derrida* (Paris: Galilée, 1984).

4 Sarah Kofman, 'The Melancholy of Art', translated by Jennifer Bajorek, in *Selected Writings*, edited by Thomas Albrecht, with Georgia Albert and Elizabeth Rottenberg (Stanford, CA: Stanford University Press, 2007), 205–17; Jacques Derrida, 'Introduction' in Kofman, *Selected Writings*, 1–34 (13), hereafter I. Derrida's eulogy was first published without a title in *Les cahiers du GRIF* 3:1 (1997), 131–66. An abridged version of the text (edited by Pascale-Anne Brault and Michael Naas) is available in *Chaque fois unique, la fin du monde* (Paris: Galilée, 2001), 205–32, and in its English translation, *The Work of Mourning* (Chicago: University of Chicago Press, 2001), 165–88. I will quote from Brault and Naas's translation of the full text available in Kofman, *Selected Writings*.

5 Penelope Deutscher, 'Pardon: Sarah Kofman and Jacques Derrida (on Mourning, Debt and Seven Friendships)', *Journal of the British Society for Phenomenology* 31:1 (2000), 21–35 (30), hereafter P.

6 Again, although a reader of Derrida would hardly be surprised that the recognition or awareness of debt is necessarily oblique, I argue that Derrida's avoidance of Kofman's proper name is uncharacteristic. One has only to remind oneself of the last page of *Dissemination* to see that an acknowledgement can both be oblique and mention proper names. See Jacques Derrida, *Dissemination*, translated by Barbara Johnson (London: Athlone Press, 1981), 366.

7 This erasure does not amount to the erasure of any woman's name in Derrida's corpus. Symmetrically to Kofman's absence, Hélène Cixous is visibly present in many of Derrida's books, whether it be as a co-author (Jacques Derrida and Hélène Cixous, *Veils*, translated by Geoffrey Bennington (Stanford, CA: Stanford University Press, 2002)), or as an author to comment on (Jacques Derrida, *H. C. for Life, That Is to Say*, translated by Laurent Milesi and Stefan Herbrechter (Stanford, CA: Stanford University Press, 2006)), in addition to being referred to in many other pieces by the philosopher (among which *Monolingualism of the Other, Or The Prosthesis of Origin*, translated by Patrick Mensah (Stanford, CA: Stanford University Press, 1998)). Let us add that Hélène Cixous also inscribed Jacques Derrida in her oeuvre, for example in *Portrait of Jacques Derrida as a Young Jewish Saint*, translated by Beverley Bic Brahic (New York: Columbia University Press, 2005). One can be struck by how differently Cixous and Kofman appear (or not) in Derrida's work, and more so because of the similitudes between the two Jewish, women writers. For more on Derrida and Cixous, see *Paragraph*, Special Issue, 'Cixous, Derrida, Psychoanalysis', edited by Mark Dawson, Mairéad Hanrahan and Eric Prenowitz, 36:2 (2013).

8 Gayatri Chakravorty Spivak, 'Love Me, Love My Ombre, Elle', *Diacritics* 14:4 (1984), 19–36 (26).

9 Not only did Kofman dedicate a very large part of her work to the history of 'woman' in Western metaphysics, but she was received and read in some quarters as a *woman* philosopher. Her inclusion in Jardine and Menke's 1988 investigation into 'French' 'Women' 'Writers', although Kofman explicitly rejects the idea of feminine writing, testifies to this reception somewhat against her will. See 'Interview with Sarah Kofman' in *Shifting Scenes*, edited by Alice A. Jardine and Ann M. Menke (New York: Columbia University Press, 1991), hereafter SS. See also Françoise Duroux, 'Comment philosophe une femme', *Les cahiers du GRIF* 3:1 (1997), 87–105, and the more recent Mathieu Frackowiak, *Sarah Kofman et le devenir-femme des philosophes* (Paris: Hermann, 2012).

10 On the question of woman in Derrida's work, see Sarah Dillon's essential contribution, 'Derrida and the Question of "Woman"' in *Derrida and Queer Theory*, edited by Christian Hite (Goleta, CA: punctum books, 2017), 108–31.

11 Although an old debate, it is still a very vivid one, and one that draws interest, as the two following pieces show: Ginette Michaud, 'Derrida and Sexual Difference' in *After Derrida: Literature, Theory and Criticism in the 21st Century*, edited by Jean-Michel Rabaté (Cambridge: Cambridge University Press, 2018), 58–79, and Anne-Emmanuelle Berger, *Queer Turn in Feminism: Identities, Sexualities, and the Theater of Gender*, translated by Catherine Porter (New York: Fordham University Press, 2014). Both study the debate between so-called constructivist feminists and essentialist feminists in relation to so-called deconstruction.

12 Alice Jardine, *Gynesis: Configurations of Woman and Modernity* (Ithaca, NY: Cornell University Press, 1985), 25, hereafter GC.

13 Françoise Collin makes similar observations in 'Le philosophe travesti ou le féminin sans les femmes', *Futur antérieur*, April 1993, https://www.multitudes.net/le-philosophe-travesti-ou-le/, consulted 27 September 2020.

14 Alice Jardine details this move in 'The Hysterical Text's Organs' in GC, 178–207.

15 Jacques Derrida, *Clang*, translated by Geoffrey Bennington and David Wills (Minneapolis, MN: University of Minnesota Press, 2021 forthcoming), 79b, hereafter C.

16 Sigmund Freud, *New Introductory Lectures*, translated by James Strachey (London: Hogarth Press, 1953–74), 132. Sarah Kofman addresses 'shame' and its typical ambivalence — at once a natural and a conventional feature — in her commentary on Rousseau, 'L'ombre de la clôture' in *Le Respect des femmes* (Paris: Galilée, 1982), 57–150.

17 See Nancy K. Miller, *Subject to Change: Reading Feminist Writing* (New York: Columbia University Press, 1988). Reading Freud's text on fetishism, we tend to privilege the second hypothesis: the female operator has vanished

from the scene, leaving only a (male) fetishist vested with a female girdle. The girdle hides his genitals, thus leaving his (and by extension, his mother's) sex undecidable. Derrida, commenting 'Fetishism' in *Clang*, interprets it as the possibility for all the sexual combinations to coexist: the mother may, or may not, be castrated.

18 Jacques Derrida, 'The Double Session' in *Dissemination*, 173–286 (175), hereafter DS. Quotation marks are Mallarmé's.

19 Jacques Derrida, *Spurs. Éperons*, translated by Barbara Harlow (Chicago and London: University of Chicago Press, 1979), 35–7, hereafter S.

20 On this question in particular, see Michaud, 'Derrida and Sexual Difference'.

21 These lines are from a one-act play by Gautier named *Pierrot posthume* (1847).

22 Sarah Kofman, *Pourquoi rit-on? Freud et le mot d'esprit* (Paris: Galilée, 1986).

23 As the provider of *toc*, 'woman' is indeed the 'mark of the critique of the proper' as Spivak argues about 'The Double Session' in 'Love Me, Love My Ombre, Elle', 22.

24 I am treading very carefully here and I shall insist that these are the *functions* of 'woman' in some of Derrida's work, and in no way the *essence* of 'woman'; as we have seen above, 'woman' does not have an essence, there are only women.

25 Sarah Kofman, 'Conjuring Death: Remarks on *The Anatomy Lesson of Doctor Nicolas Tulp* (1632)', translated by Pascale-Anne Brault, in *Selected Writings*, 237–41 (239), hereafter CD.

26 Pascale-Anne Brault quotes from Blanchot's *The Madness of the Day*, translated by George Quasha, in *The Station Hill Blanchot Reader* (Barrytown, NY: Station Hill Press, 1981), 7.

27 Jacques Derrida, 'Choreographies', translated by Christie McDonald, *Diacritics* 12:2 (1982), 66–76 (76).

28 Jacques Derrida, *Cinders*, translated by Ned Lukacher (Lincoln, NE: University of Nebraska Press, 1991).

29 Jacques Derrida, *The Post Card: From Socrates to Freud and Beyond*, translated by Alan Bass (Chicago: University of Chicago Press, 1987), 53. The gender indeterminacy of the protagonists of *The Post Card* is discussed by Spivak in 'Love Me, Love My Ombre, Elle', 26f.

30 Catherine Malabou, *Changing Difference: The Feminine and the Question of Philosophy*, translated by Carolyn Shread (Cambridge, UK and Malden, MA: Polity Press, 2011), 107. The last essay of the book from which this citation is taken is particularly relevant to our argument here and we take the liberty of referring the reader to it.

31 Sarah Kofman, 'Subvertir le philosophique ou Pour un supplément de jouissance' [interview with Evelyne Ender], *Compar(a)ison* 1 (1993), 9–26 (16).

Sarah Kofman and the Allure of Music

COSMIN TOMA

According to a recent neurological study, musical anhedonia, a condition where one derives little to no pleasure from exposure to music, affects approximately 3–5% of the world's population.[1] This means that at least 95% of us savour music to some degree, cementing its status as perhaps the most beloved Muse of all. Music can thus be said to possess a nigh-universal *allure*, as may likewise be inferred from the numerous Greek myths that describe its spellbinding, even maddening power. Whether it be the tale of Orpheus, whose songful lyre sways even the dead denizens of Tartarus, or that of Marsyas, the satyr who challenged the god Apollo to a musical duel only to be flayed alive for his insolence, music is routinely depicted as an instrument of emotive persuasion, even of torture, as Pascal Quignard eloquently demonstrated in *The Hatred of Music*.[2] Indeed, music is a two-faced Muse, whose charms are owed in no small part to its duplicitous nature. As such, there is no deep-seated contradiction between Apollo's divine portfolio as keeper of harmonic order — guardian of the music of the spheres — and his Dionysian rage at being compelled to acknowledge his rival's musical talent. And it is this very two-facedness — between relief as incantatory consolation and relief as violent foregrounding — that characterizes the presence of music in Sarah Kofman's work, which is at once persistent and discreet, quite unlike that of the visual arts, which are more immediately visible in her bibliography.

Three strands or movements of unequal length will be explored here, each of which will touch upon a specific volume of Kofman's: *Nietzsche and Metaphor*, *L'Imposture de la beauté* (which has yet to be translated into English and whose title I am tempted to render, somewhat flippantly, as *Beauty Is a Sham*) and, lastly, *Rue Ordener, rue Labat*. Although the topic of music is also incidentally discussed in *Autobiogriffures*, I will not attend to it here, as the first two titles

Paragraph 44.1 (2021): 73–87
DOI: 10.3366/para.2021.0355

www.euppublishing.com/para

more thoroughly testify to her understanding of the art of sounds — via Nietzsche, above all — while the third affords us a rare glimpse into her autobiographical relationship with music and, more broadly, the experience of writing. We shall thus see how her interpretations of Nietzsche's writings on music are almost paradigmatically neutral in their readerly fidelity to the originals, whereas *Rue Ordener, rue Labat* suggests a more emotionally charged rapport with music. In closing, I shall consider the possibility that these two, ostensibly divergent modes of reading and writing are very much in tune with each other.

★

Let us begin, then, with *Nietzsche and Metaphor*.[3] This is no accident, of course. Not only because it marks, alongside *The Childhood of Art*, the beginning of Kofman's published oeuvre but also because it is impossible to write convincingly, exhaustively and pedagogically on Nietzsche, as Kofman does in this book, without attending to his passion for music.

In her 2002 essay *La Musique en respect* (Music at a Respectful Distance), Marie-Louise Mallet reminds us that music is something of a nocturnal enigma for philosophy, which it leaves at a loss for words; according to Nietzsche, whom she quotes, it is 'an art of night and twilight'.[4] As Jean-Luc Nancy and Philippe Lacoue-Labarthe have also respectively noted, music represents a challenge for philosophy, to which the *logos* is tempted to respond by tearing the musician to shreds or, at the very least, by turning a deaf ear to their tune.[5] And against this age-old logocentric backdrop, Nietzsche's uncommon fascination with music is thrown into sharp relief, to such an extent that even the philosophical and/or rhetorical problem of metaphor as it manifests itself in his work cannot be scrutinized without reference to the art of sounds.

Kofman is keenly aware of this. Notwithstanding the first chapter — in fact, a short introduction — which subtly alludes to aural matters by describing Nietzsche's philosophy as 'inouïe et insolente' (literally, 'unheard-of and insolent' (N, 6)), the second chapter's first section bears the title 'Music, the Privileged Art'.[6] In it, she summarizes Nietzsche's own retelling of the origin of language in *The Birth of Tragedy*, where he argues, in keeping with William Warburton, Étienne Bonnot de Condillac and Jean-Jacques Rousseau, that the true fault of logocentrism (this is admittedly anachronistic but no less relevant for it) is that it is not phonocentric and otocentric enough.[7] Nietzsche thus distinguishes between the word's abstract conceptuality and its primitive poetry, presumed to be the province of musical organs: the vocal tract, with its ability to produce wordless sounds, and the ear, which in *Daybreak* he describes as the seat of 'fear' (D, 143), an all-consuming, substratal emotion that overwhelms us in the dead of night, when sight subsides and hearing takes over. In other words, Nietzsche attempts to account for what lies beyond philosophy's ken (which is, in fact, a characteristically philosophical, even metaphysical gesture) by arguing *contra* philosophy.

As Kofman succinctly reminds us, 'Nietzsche judges the conceptual language of philosophy the most inappropriate to express the "truth of the world", since it is at three removes from it, simply a metaphor for a metaphor' (N, 6). She goes on to specify that 'we can have only representations of the essence of things, since we ourselves, and the universe along with us, are only images of this completely "indecipherable" innermost essence' (N, 6). At the heart of it all, then, lies some unfathomable thing that is not so much inexpressible as it is a cipher or a crypt. What is more, this crypt has no truth to disclose; it is not an encrypted code that one may cannily learn to decrypt. Its secret may only be evoked or *suggested*, which is to say that the secret must be kept.[8] And as it so happens, 'the most appropriate representation of the innermost essence of things' (N, 7), to quote Kofman quoting and paraphrasing Nietzsche, who in turn is paraphrasing Schopenhauer, is music. Insofar as it is 'a necessary "supplement" to words, which are "the most defective signs there are"' (N, 7), music purportedly comes closest to imparting something of that crypt or secret.

On this account, even lyric poetry is but an 'Apollinian metaphor for Dionysian music', and 'the lyric poet, who can perceive himself only through the prism of music, can express nothing which was not already there in the music to an extraordinary degree' (N, 8). While this recalls Rousseau's noted *mélomanie*, Nietzsche's hierarchical model further radicalizes that of the *Essay on the Origin of Languages* in that speech and melody are no longer viewed from the vantage point of consubstantiality; rather, the metaphorical 'essence' of all things requires that they remain distinct, differentiated and hence given over to *différance avant la lettre.*[9] Indeed, Nietzsche, like many other German thinkers and writers of his time, tends to conceive of music as an autonomous art, one that risks being vitiated by misguided synæsthetic attempts at translating sound into image, which would be tantamount to 'substitut[ing] the son for the father, man for god' (N, 9). Although

Kofman here is glossing an early work, *The Birth of Tragedy*, she points out that

> This is what Nietzsche will later condemn in the music of Wagner: as a musician he was a rhetorician, making the music serve the text and seeking above all to be 'expressive', to give a commentary on an idea using a thousand symbols. (N, 10)

Put differently, Wagner was not enough of a *musician*, hence the subtitle of *The Case of Wagner*, which refers to him as a mere *Musikant*, a minstrel or street musician.

Conversely, for the philosopher — Sarah Nietzsche and/or Friedrich Kofman, as it were, so thorough is her identification with him in *Nietzsche and Metaphor*, which faithfully records his thoughts on the topic, as though to *replay* and even *remix* them — music is perhaps the greatest metaphor of all. Its mercurial essence is so utterly metaphorical and supplemental as to border on the metaphor-in-itself or the supplement-in-itself; it is the idiom that comes closest to opening the unutterable, indecipherable crypt which, for Nietzsche, is nothing less than life itself. Aside from its hyperbolic bent, which testifies to the enrapturing allure music is capable of exerting, it is a perilously paradoxical stance, one that risks slipping back into the metaphysical and conceptual discourse that Nietzsche is ever-intent on subverting. After all, why insist on condemning so-called '[o]peratic culture' (N, 10) if the quest for a *Gesamtkunstwerk* or total artwork is doomed to fail from the get-go? In other words, why not view opera as a tragic exacerbation of our metaphorical condition, a fascinating demonstration of the impossibility of conceptual oneness, a bundle of engrossing fragments? Why seek a one-to-one correspondence between metaphor and metaphor, a degree of authenticity that is ultimately at odds with the artifice of art? Why not let the lie (be a) lie?

Although Kofman herself does not address this facet of the problematic head on, perhaps out of fidelity to Nietzsche, the German philosopher's own position is all the stranger when one considers his ostensible contempt for the music of Wagner's rival, Johannes Brahms, who was famously championed by Eduard Hanslick, a noted nineteenth-century critic and advocate for so-called absolute music.[10] Indeed, Nietzsche argues in *The Case of Wagner* that Brahms's 'good fortune was a German misunderstanding: he was taken for Wagner's antagonist' because 'an antagonist was *needed*'.[11] This, Nietzsche claims (no doubt playing up the antagonism himself), accounts for the absence of 'necessity' that underpins Brahms's music, which expresses nothing but 'the melancholy of impotence' (W, 187).[12] Worse yet, Brahms 'is the musician for a certain type of dissatisfied women' (W, 187), who merely *yearn* for abundance rather than exude it. For these reasons and more besides, Brahms's music is thus supposedly devoid of the snappy, rhythmic virility Nietzsche ascribes to the superior composer-creator.

Despite all that stands between them, then, Brahms and Wagner are both too Teutonic, each in his own way. Their compositions fall short of the *gai saber*, to cite the original Provençal expression, that presumably drives Georges Bizet's *Carmen*, Nietzsche's favourite opera, which he saw performed more than twenty times, bespeaking a veritable obsession. 'This music', he writes, 'seems perfect to me. It approaches lightly, supplely, politely. It is pleasant, it does not *sweat*. (...) Bizet makes me fertile. Whatever is good makes me fertile' (W, 157–8). Here it needs to be said — to Nietzsche's credit, assuming we wish him to be at all self-consistent — that he does not treat *Carmen* as the opera it purports to be but rather as a piece of music whose narrative elements are, in fact, superfluous or secondary at best.[13] Yet this does not prevent him from praising Bizet's work on ideological grounds, as though it were of utmost importance that it match his own philosophical aims — 'The return to nature, health, cheerfulness, youth, *virtue*!' — which he contrasts with the key themes of 'devotion', 'loyalty' and 'purity' peddled by Wagner, that 'clever rattlesnake' (W, 159–60). Indeed, as Kofman would later write, mimicking Nietzsche once again, *Carmen* is 'a drama affirming life in all of its cruelty and sensuality, one that returns love to its rightful place in nature and in life'.[14]

If music must of necessity stand for something else, if it 'breaks up into a thousand metaphors' (N, 11), then the composer's role is to ensure that the 'right' metaphors (which tellingly happen to be the most *musical*, according to Nietzsche) come into relief. Fragmentation is inevitable and even desirable — hence the Nietzschean corpus's own disembodiment — but the end goal remains the rebirth of Dionysus, the truest and most archetypal name for 'life'. This is also why, as Kofman writes, 'only the full panoply of the arts in their hierarchized diversity subordinated to music (...) symbolizes Dionysus: this god who is dismembered into a thousand pieces and who revives every year, reunified' (N, 12). Aesthetic synthesis therefore remains an object of desire, especially if it harks back to the Greek model of old, but on one condition: that music reign supreme, foremost in its proximity to, and complicity with, the indecipherable:

> In the drama, each art can serve another as its metaphorical expression: the movements of the chorists, who draw arabesques on the stage, make the music, as it were, visible, just as the music reinforces the daring metaphors and the leaps of thought which are given in the poem. But it was music alone that gave birth to tragic myth, which expresses in symbols the Dionysian truths, just as only the full panoply of the arts expresses Dionysus. (N, 13)

Before moving on to Kofman's other writings on music, it bears noting that here, as elsewhere in *Nietzsche and Metaphor*, she appears to be committed to shadowing the German philosopher's chain of argumentation to a remarkable extent, as though she were tasked with 'performing' or 'playing' his texts in order to do them justice, thus granting special weight to her claim (in fact, Nietzsche's) that 'for the artist to be able to symbolize Dionysus in this way he must first have been metamorphosed and stripped of his individuality himself' and that 'It is this ecstasy outside of the self which is at the origin of Greek music drama' (N, 12). As such, the tremendous sense of identification that underlies the book in its entirety may itself be a Dionysian, metaphorically *musical* gesture, even in this most academic of contexts (after all, the book was initially conceived as a doctoral thesis).

★

Some twenty years later, Kofman revisits the same musical scene in a piece entitled 'Nietzsche et Wagner. Comment la musique devient bonne pour les cochons' (Nietzsche and Wagner: How Music Becomes Fit for Pigs), which was soon to be reprinted in *L'Imposture de la beauté*.[15] Although there is no extant English translation of the volume in its entirety, 'Nietzsche et Wagner' is available in English under the rather more scholarly title of 'Wagner's Ascetic Ideal According to Nietzsche'.

From the outset, Kofman warns us that her essay will not be an exhaustive survey of Nietzsche and Wagner's relationship. Rather, it aims to provide a close 'reading of the first few paragraphs of the Third Essay of *On the Genealogy of Morals*' (WA, 193). In line with her method of reading as 'inhabitation', she approaches the philosopher–composer couple not so much from Nietzsche's perspective — in sympathy with his spirit, as it were — as from that of his writing, nearly to the letter, stressing the written word above all.

In a context where musical considerations are at stake, this is hardly trivial.[16] Indeed, Kofman — much like Nietzsche himself, in fact — appears to be exclusively interested in the philosophical content that may be gleaned from Wagner's operas, making no overt attempt to engage with the more immediately musical facet of his aesthetic.

To some extent, Wagner is responsible for the remarkable ease with which one may discuss his work without lending it so much as an ear (and this holds true even before we delve into his notorious anti-Semitism). As Kofman sardonically points out in her summary of Nietzsche's position, 'Wagner made of music a simple medium subordinated to drama: a simple woman who needed a man in order to blossom' (WA, 206). For the German composer, art does not aspire towards the condition of music; rather, it is a mere vehicle whose role is to be subsumed in the *Gesamtkunstwerk*, which is at heart a mere spectacle, and hence a decadent parody of true art, if Nietzsche is to be believed.[17] It is a 'perversion', even, to recall the term that Kofman uses in the third subheading of her piece. In deploying music 'only to accentuate, reinforce, and internalize the dramatic gesture and surface of the actor' and in arguing 'again and again that his music signifies more than just music', Wagner thus exhibits a 'perverted taste' (WA, 206). Put differently, Wagner's operas lack the right kind of relief: they do not foreground music as they should, preferring instead to focus on framing devices, be they of a verbal, visual or theatrical nature.

Yet beyond Nietzsche's lack of interest in Brahms, whether real or feigned, he was also explicitly opposed, as Kofman reminds us, to 'art for art's sake', which cannot be 'the distinctive feature of a flourishing art' (WA, 207). Indeed, Kofman writes that 'In an aphorism entitled "*L'art pour l'art*" in *Twilight* (TI IX:24), Nietzsche shows how the phrase "art for art's sake" (. . .) is simply a reversal of the opposite phrase, and in fact signifies the power of moral judgment' (WA, 207), for it all too heavily relies on its dialectical partner, namely an art whose justifications are external to itself. Instead, there is a third, more essential term that takes over from the other two: *life* as such, once again, in all of its indecipherable and dynamic glory.

Here too, music is consequently more than 'just' music for Nietzsche. On the one hand, the art of sounds is compelled to transcend itself in order to convey the rhythmic energy of life; on the other hand, it becomes one with life in the process, to such an extent that to speak of music is to speak of life and the obverse, as there is no simple distinction to be drawn here between the thing-in-itself and its idiom. Yet even this alloy does not quite satisfy Nietzsche, who calls for the purportedly a-conceptual concept of life to be put into greater relief still, relegating music to the background in the process.

In truth, Nietzsche's increasing contempt for Wagner, with whom he has far more in common than first meets the eye, more readily hinges on the latter's espousal of a different kind of relief altogether, namely Schopenhauerian consolation. According to Nietzsche, Wagner conflates relief with asceticism and therefore parodies the vital will by reducing it to a will unto nothingness, especially in his later works, which reach their apotheosis in *Parsifal.* Although the notion of 'relief' is never named as such in Kofman's essay (nor does it carry quite the same polysemous meaning in French), her Freudian insistence on the medical aspects of Nietzsche's reading of Wagner speaks to this very concern. Indeed, the paragraph that introduces this facet of the matter deserves to be quoted in full:

> The example of Wagner is a 'case' with which Nietzsche, doctor *par excellence* of famous diagnostic skills, has been very familiar for quite some time. He has often been consulted regarding this patient (*on l'a souvent consulté sur ce malade*), who himself professes to be the right physician for cases of hysteria. Doctor Nietzsche, however, for his part, defends an opposing view: to wit, that this patient is a most nefarious danger to the health of women and young people. Has the doctor 'been' consulted? (*'On' l'a consulté?*) Well, rather, he consulted himself; for behind the case of Wagner, and furthermore that of Socrates (between which cases multiple parallels could be drawn), lies the case of Nietzsche: of the mad admiration he first manifested for Wagner, whom, in the correspondence of his early period, he calls his master and father, and to whom, in the manner of a dutiful son, he never failed to send birthday greetings; and then of the final rejection, marked in *The Case of Wagner* and *Nietzsche Contra Wagner* by Wagner's reduction to a typical artist of decadence — a veritable calamity for music, who sickens all that he touches. (WA, 196)

Among the multiple figures of relief that may be distilled from this passage — so multiple, in fact, that they recall the Derridean *pharmakon*'s infinite versatility — there is relief from the influence exerted by a past idol, relief from one's own misguided suspension of disbelief, relief from the eldritch intensity of art, relief from philosophy, relief from the father, and of course Wagner's own attempt at relieving Bayreuth's pilgrims of the travails of modern life.[18] Above all, there is the desire of relief from Wagner's sickening touch (which relieves *of* life, as it were) and hence the will to escape the state of morbid fascination into which he lures his listeners. Such indeed is the allure of music, whose Circe-like, perverting power is greater than one may know, possessing the ability to turn the listener into a pig, which is exactly how the Odysseus-like Nietzsche views Wagner's admirers.

Parsifal in particular is the work of an impotent old man who has stooped so low as to take refuge in the bloodless promises of Christianity. 'Wagner, in the end was converted', writes Kofman, who stresses that 'He began to believe in oppositions and became a pessimist' (WA, 201). Belief in binaries is thus openly condemned as an instance of facile relief, and Nietzsche is no doubt also thinking here of his own early claim, in *The Birth of Tragedy*, that art is split between two contradictory impulses: the Apollonian and the Dionysian. Yet, as Kofman readily shows us, one cannot argue that Nietzsche has seriously overcome diametrical oppositions, so vehement is he in his disavowal of Wagner's music. The conversion thus occurs both ways: just as the erstwhile sanguine composer has become an austere Christian who rejects life, so the philosopher is now a joyful anti-Wagnerian, whose stance is all the more legitimate, having experienced the allure of Wagner's music from within. In other words, he is still reeling from a past identification; the Sirens' song is still echoing in his ears.

And it is the problem of identification in particular that concerns Kofman in her closing paragraphs, which also happen to be most overtly 'critical' with regard to Nietzsche, marking a break with the seemingly neutral stance she had espoused up until that point. Indeed, she asks:

> Does not the vague impulse of the decadent artist to identify with his characters, in order to feel 'real,' equally apply to Nietzsche? And in speaking of Wagner, was Nietzsche ever speaking of anyone other than himself? Did he not spend his life identifying with Wagner, Schopenhauer, Heraclitus, Empedocles, with all the historical figures who are all fictions, characters of his own creation?
>
> (. . .)
>
> But didn't the multiplicity of identifications lead rather to a radical dispossession — to what one calls Nietzsche's madness? (WA, 208–9)

To this litany of rhetorical questions, one may add the following echoes: what of Kofman herself? To what extent is her piece about Nietzsche? About Wagner? About music? About philosophy? About psychoanalysis? About something else entirely? And is the present piece about her? About Nietzsche? About Wagner? About myself? About Dionysus? Or another still? Who identifies with whom, or with what, in this web where everything is a metaphor, where each thing stands for another, where one is 'metamorphosed and stripped of his individuality' (N, 12), where it is precisely music that leads one to pursue these interrogations in the first place? What is it that exerts its allure here, that draws one towards the other, like the *Blumenmädchen* or Flowermaidens whose sole *raison d'être* in *Parsifal* is to lure and enthral the Grail Knights and hence to embody the fascination of which music and art are uniquely capable?

★

Instead of providing a *direct* answer to any of these questions, I would now like to briefly turn to *Rue Ordener, rue Labat* and discuss how music innerves Kofman's writing in this autobiographical *récit*.[19] First, an observation: if we provisionally allow that the musicality of a given prose style lies somewhere between Virginia Woolf's *The Waves* and the denotational naming of composers and/or musical compositions, *Rue Ordener, rue Labat* is surely nearer to the latter end of the spectrum. Although it raises, from the very beginning, the question of style — indeed, the phrase 'De lui, il me reste seulement le stylo' ('Of him all I have left is the fountain pen') subtly gestures towards it — Kofman approaches the matter in psychoanalytic rather than in musical terms.[20] In other words, finding the right wording or phrasing for 'ça' ('it' or the 'id') is a task that cannot be left to the aesthetic devices of music (timbre, harmony, melody, rhythm, etc.), as emphasized by the recurrent use of quotation marks around certain terms such as '"ramassé"' ('"picked up"') (RO, 11/5 and 23/17), which happens to be *le mot juste* for reasons having more to do with history than with art. Yet the Greek lament 'ô popoï, popoï, popoï', which Kofman poetically scans as 'ô papa, papa, papa' (RO, 14/7), is no stranger to the music of rhythm, and constitutes a dirge unto itself.

Of her father Bereck Kofman, Sarah obviously retains more than just the fountain pen: 'We would spend', she writes, 'the last hours of the day together in his room singing Hebrew songs and others whose words he had made up himself', thus tying verbal invention to song, before adding: 'later I recognized one of the tunes in a symphony by Gustav Mahler' (RO, 11/5). And this proper name, which simultaneously denotes her acquisition of highbrow culture via the influence of Mémé (a classical music enthusiast) and her Jewish roots (Mahler, an Austrian Jew, is well known for incorporating Jewish melodies into his compositions), is, in fact, the first of many in the *récit* — names of writers, for the most part, but Beethoven is also cited as the epitome of 'la "grande musique"' (RO, 59/48 and 99/84), since he was Mémé's favourite composer.[21] Music resounds here by way of metonymy, and even though no Beethoven or Mahler compositions are mentioned as such, one may hear the outline of their respective signature styles as soon as their names are inscribed.

Yet there is another named musician here: Sarah Kofman herself, who recalls how, during her stay in Moissac as a young girl, she 'sang in the chorus and played the flute' (RO, 94/80), a rather striking gloss insofar as it indirectly brings to mind an earlier anecdote pertaining to her elementary school teacher, Madame Fagnard: 'She made us forget about the air raid and our fright by having us sing or play games or by telling us stories like the rather disturbing *Pied Piper of Hamelin* to distract our attention from the immediate danger' (RO, 25–6/19).[22]

Seemingly giving the lie to the 'neutral' identification Kofman appears to be performing, in a quasi-musical sense, in her writings on Nietzsche, this composite image, which slowly emerges as one reads *Rue Ordener, rue Labat*, is nothing less than haunting: the young Sarah Kofman in the midst of an air raid during World War II, raptly listening to the unsettling tale of the Pied Piper of Hamelin, tuning into the song of a silent flute made of words, basking in a terrifying musical lure meant to provide relief from the terror of reality, then later, many pages later, learning to play the instrument herself, 'until the day [she] dropped it by accident from [her] window on the second floor into the Tarn River' (RO, 94/80).

⋆

In closing, let us stay with this likeness, which lies somewhere between the contiguous realms of words and music: Sarah Kofman as pied piper or *joueuse de flûte*, compelled to pick up the instrument by a verbal retelling of its diabolical charms then absent-mindedly relinquishing its power, perhaps for the sake of its immediate rival, the pen, which in turn immortalizes the musical instrument through a *récit*, which happens to be *Rue Ordener, rue Labat*.[23] There are countless ways of parsing this scene, but I will only throw one of its visible facets into relief here: Kofman as *interprète*.

That this angle should require the French language is no accident. As a general rule, the English 'interpreter' is neither a reader nor a writer per se. In most cases, an interpreter is a conversational translator, one who is tasked with finding spoken linguistic equivalents, without recourse to the written word. This definition holds true in French as well, but it also carries an array of additional meanings: commentator, hermeneut, actor, singer, mouthpiece, performer, player, and so on, thus touching not only on the art of reading but also on the arts in general and music in particular. To 'interpret' a score is therefore to *perform* it, blurring the lines between these seemingly distinct activities, which is precisely what Kofman does whenever she 'inhabits' (I am quoting Penelope Deutscher, once again) a given text or even an author, starting with Nietzsche and Freud. This is not to say that the *interprète* has no agency — as the above-cited rhetorical questions from her chapter on Nietzsche and Wagner demonstrate, Kofman is very much aware of the pitfalls of performative identification, which she tellingly underscores in a context where music is at stake — but a certain degree of fidelity to the score is canonically assumed to be a prerequisite for playing such works, and it is this often subversive interpretive and performative fidelity that lies at the core of Kofman's approach to commentary.

To illustrate this, we may return, one last time, to *Nietzsche and Metaphor*. When Kofman entitles the first chapter 'An Unheard-of and Insolent Philosophy', her reference to hearing is quite remarkable insofar as the ensuing analysis specifically focuses on the challenge posed by writing *on* Nietzsche. In other words, part of the problem that invariably arises when one is tasked with glossing Nietzsche's fragmentary oeuvre is that of *listening* in the sense of *entente*, which implies that understanding is a matter of sounds and/or soundness, as well as of negotiation and dialogue. Yet the business of interpretive performance or *interprétation* far exceeds mere repetition, that is obedience understood as *ob audire* (hearing-to and hence conforming to the object of hearing). Indeed, 'being faithful to Nietzsche does not mean doing as he does, writing as he does. This would be an impossible task, one which would imply the existence of an absolute norm of "good taste" and good style, an imperative which everyone would have to obey' (N, 2), as she writes from the very outset. There is thus a sense in which to obey Nietzsche is to disobey him, to turn one's hearing away from his words, between or beyond them, which is where reading as *interprétation* can begin. It implies a readerly experience of hearing that interprets the so-called source material as a latent score awaiting performance.

It may be said that Kofman was preternaturally in tune with her subjects — Nietzsche and Freud above all — and that, through her writing, she was a writer–composer's ideal *interprète* insofar as her performances appear to be more 'self-effacing' than those of her (male) peers. Yet as every classical music fan intimately knows, there is no such thing as a 'neutral' performance of a given work; the greatest semblance of transparency does more to expose a composition's more or less secret quirks and flaws than overt showmanship aimed at drawing attention to the player. Put differently, bringing a composed piece into relief always implies some measure of violence, on the *interprète*'s part, even when discretion appears to be the guiding principle. Such, perhaps, is the metaphorical lure and allure of music as a critical reading — and writing — practice in Sarah Kofman's work.

NOTES

1 Ernest Mas-Herrero, Josep Marco-Pallarés, Urbano Lorenzo-Seva, Robert J. Zatorre and Antoni Rodriguez-Fornells, 'Individual Differences in Music Reward Experiences', *Music Perception* 31:2 (2013), 118–38.

2 Pascal Quignard, *The Hatred of Music*, translated by Matthew Amos and Fredrik Rönnbäck (New Haven, CT and London: Yale University Press, 2016).

3 Sarah Kofman, *Nietzsche and Metaphor*, translated by Duncan Large (Stanford, CA: Stanford University Press, 1994), hereafter N.

4 Marie-Louise Mallet, *La Musique en respect* (Paris: Galilée, 2002); Friedrich Nietzsche, *Daybreak: Thoughts on the Prejudices of Morality*, translated by J. R. Hollingdale, edited by Maudemarie Clark and Brian Leiter (Cambridge: Cambridge University Press, 1997), 253, hereafter D.

5 See Jean-Luc Nancy, *Listening*, translated by Charlotte Mandell (New York: Fordham University Press, 2007), and Philippe Lacoue-Labarthe, *Pour n'en pas finir: écrits sur la musique* (Paris: Christian Bourgois, 2015).

6 Sarah Kofman, *Nietzsche et la métaphore* (Paris: Galilée, 1983), 13.

7 Friedrich Nietzsche, *The Birth of Tragedy*, translated by Douglas Smith (Oxford and New York: Oxford University Press, 2000).

8 I am deeply indebted to Ginette Michaud for having so eloquently brought this insight out into the open. See Ginette Michaud, *Tenir au secret (Derrida Blanchot)* (Paris: Galilée, 2006), and *Battements du secret littéraire* (*Lire Jacques Derrida et Hélène Cixous*, vol. I) (Paris: Hermann, 2010).

9 It goes without saying that much of *Nietzsche and Metaphor* can be fruitfully read via Kofman's dialogue with Jacques Derrida, particularly the latter's 'White Mythology: Metaphor in the Text of Philosophy', in *Margins of Philosophy*, translated by Alan Bass (Chicago: University of Chicago Press, 1982), 207–72. For an in-depth discussion of this encounter, see Ginette Michaud and Isabelle Ullern, *Sarah Kofman et Jacques Derrida: croisements, écarts, différences* (Paris: Hermann, 2018).

10 See Eduard Hanslick, *On the Musically Beautiful: A Contribution Towards the Revision of the Aesthetics of Music*, translated by Geoffrey Payzant (Indianapolis, IN: Hackett, 1986).

11 Friedrich Nietzsche, 'The Case of Wagner' in *The Birth of Tragedy and The Case of Wagner*, translated by Walter Kaufmann (New York: Vintage Books, 1967), 187, hereafter W.

12 Kaufmann translates 'Melancholie des Unvermögens' as 'melancholy of incapacity'.

13 Maurice Blanchot, in particular, relentlessly stressed the irreducibly fragmentary dimension of Nietzsche's writings. See, for instance, Maurice Blanchot, *The Infinite Conversation*, translated by Susan Hanson (Minneapolis, MN and London: University of Minnesota Press, 1993).

14 Sarah Kofman, 'Wagner's Ascetic Ideal According to Nietzsche', translated by David Blacker and Jessica George, revised by Alban Urbanas and by the editor and Judith Rowan, in *Nietzsche, Genealogy, Morality: Essays on Nietzsche's* Genealogy of Morals, edited by Richard Schacht (Berkeley, CA: University of California Press, 1994), 199, hereafter WA.

15 Sarah Kofman, *L'Imposture de la beauté* (Paris: Galilée, 1995).

16 Penelope Deutscher rightly foregrounds this term, which goes a long way towards elucidating the kind of reading that Kofman undertakes. See Penelope Deutscher, 'The Feminine as What Kind of Problem?', translated into French by Cosmin Toma as 'Le féminin, quel genre de question?', in *Sarah Kofman: philosopher autrement* (Paris: Hermann) (forthcoming).

17 As per Walter Pater's famous dictum according to which 'All art constantly aspires towards the condition of music'. Walter Pater, *The Renaissance: Studies in Art and Poetry* (Berkeley and Los Angeles, CA and London: University of California Press, 1980), 106.

18 See Jacques Derrida, 'Plato's Pharmacy' in *Dissemination*, translated by Barbara Johnson (London and New York: Continuum, 2004), 67–186.

19 This untranslatable term, which simultaneously means story, tale, narrative and account, shall remain untranslated.

20 Sarah Kofman, *Rue Ordener, rue Labat* (Paris: Galilée, 1994), 3, and Sarah Kofman, *Rue Ordener, Rue Labat*, translated by Ann Smock (Lincoln, NE: University of Nebraska Press, 1996), 3, hereafter RO; page numbers are to the French-language edition followed by the English-language edition. Interestingly, the French version refers to *Le Charmeur de rats de Hamelin*, which is slightly closer to the German original (*Rattenfänger von Hamelin*, or The Rat Catcher of Hamelin) than the more ubiquitous *Le Joueur de flûte de Hamelin* (The Flute Player of Hamelin), in line with the English title in that it underscores the musical instrument itself.

21 Editors' note: Mémé, or 'the lady of Rue Labat', is a prominent figure in Kofman's 'autobiographical *récit*', *Rue Ordener, rue Labat*. For further detail on this figure in this volume, see this volume's articles by Duncan Large and Joseph Johnson.

22 It must be said here, however, that between the German *Pfeife*, the English 'pipe' and the French *flûte*, there is a subtle organological taxonomy that, in its own way, speaks to the difficulty, even the impossibility of rendering instrumental timbre via linguistic matter.

23 In the introduction to *Un métier impossible* ((Paris: Galilée, 1983), 27–9), Kofman incidentally evokes Freud's parallel between the analysand's psyche and a musical instrument — in fact, a flute — which the analyst must learn to play well in order to draw 'beautiful sounds' from the analysand instead of torturing them.

The Margins of a Nightmare

JOSEPH R. JOHNSON

Introduction: Kofman's Literary Clinic

Although Sarah Kofman indicated as early as 1976 that she 'always wanted to recount (her) life', the act seemed to come with difficulty.[1] Compared with the voluminous nature of Kofman's philosophical output, her three initial forays into life-writing appeared infrequently, taking lacunary forms. Framed as non-philosophical reflections, each of these essays finds Kofman employing a kind of detour to narrativize her personal experience: in 'Tomb for a Proper Name', a dream provides the opportunity for autobiographical reflection by de-naturalizing the spelling of her name; in '"My Life" and Psychoanalysis', Kofman's own analytic experience plays the same role; in 'Sacrée nourriture' ('Damned Food'), it is instead a memory of the incompatible culinary pressures to which she was subjected by Mémé (who insisted on the consumption of red meat, including pork) and her biological mother (who upheld the ritual preparation of food according to Jewish law).[2] Yet each of these essays of fewer than 500 words also cites an impasse, a block in the act of recounting: in the first case, the 'double castration' (TP, 249) encoded into the materiality of her own name; in the second, an inability to sustain a linear narrative of life events while maintaining an affective connection to those same events; in the third, the pain of a 'double bind' (DF, 248) with no possibility of escape.[3]

1983's *Comment s'en sortir?* ('Beyond Aporia?') marked a shift from this practice: here for the first time, life-writing emerges as if it were the natural outcome of philosophical reflection.[4] For the majority of the short book, Kofman works within her usual frame of deconstructive, philosophical discourse, guiding readers through a close analysis of the term *aporia* in Plato's dialogues. *Aporia*, Kofman writes, is untranslatable (CSS, 17/BA, 9); usual translations

Paragraph 44.1 (2021): 88–102
DOI: 10.3366/para.2021.0356

www.euppublishing.com/para

as something to the effect of 'unresolvable contradiction' mask a complicated poetic resonance in Ancient Greek linking the term to specific situations that elicit hopelessness and despair. As Socrates reveals in the *Republic* during a debate over the proper nature of women's education, an aporetic situation is a state of being lost-at-sea; to hope for a way out of the dilemma, a *poros*, is to be like one who jumps overboard in the middle of the ocean and hopes to come across a rescuing dolphin or 'some other impossible means of salvation [*aporon sotèrian*]'.[5] This 'genuine miracle' (CSS, 25/BA, 12) condenses the philosophical-affective dilemma at the centre of the text: for one who has fallen into an aporia, to hope to *s'en sortir* is to hope for a miracle, since no one actually possesses the *poros*, even if everyone in an aporia desires it (CSS, 53).[6]

As if in recognition of this problem's unresolvable nature, the final chapter of *Comment s'en sortir?* appears to drop the question of the *aporia* and the *poros* entirely. Titled 'Nightmare: At the Margins of Medieval Studies', this unexpected conclusion finds Kofman delving into the field of medieval philology, a subject never before broached in any of her previous works. Kofman relates that while reading a book by the celebrated medievalist Bernard Cerquiglini called *La Parole médiévale*, she became inspired by a section on the Old French particle *mar*, a lexeme that resists conventional etymological explanation, grammatical classification and modern translation all at once.[7] Thought to have been derived from the Latin *mala hora* — the evil hour, *malheur*, misfortune and unhappiness — the uses of this highly idiomatic medieval French term encompassed many different contexts of struggle and suffering; it offered a formalized means of expressing grief, an almost theatrical sense of inconsolability.[8] At this point, it becomes possible to see that the medieval adverb marks the development, rather than abandonment, of Kofman's preceding arguments: *mar* functions as a counterpoint and response to the vanished terms *aporia* and *poros*. One untranslatable term referring to the nature of an aporetic situation (*aporia*) fades into an equally untranslatable new term (*mar*) whose ill-defined contours mirror those of the aporia itself: just as aporias are 'radically other' (CSS, 98), *mar* occupies 'the very heart of alterity' (quoted in CSS, 105/NM, 252). However, because its theatrical, formulaic utterance allows for the *expression* of suffering within an aporetic situation, *mar* can be thought to offer a provisional sort of *poros* as well; this connection is subtly foreshadowed by Kofman's earlier characterization of *poroi* as '*mar*itime routes of passage' and as 'the resource of sailors [*marins*]' (CSS, 20/BA, 10, emphasis mine).

Apparently as a consequence of the medieval adverb's unique power to give an 'orderly form' to the 'expression of misfortune' (CSS, 108/NM, 253), Kofman's analysis of *mar* heralds an intensely personal turn in the book's final pages. Just as uttering *mar* might in medieval literature have enabled a soldier to mourn a fallen comrade, or allowed a feminine lyric voice to express her hopelessness in love (CSS, 107/NM, 253; see PM, 133), the active and creative use of this term seems to offer Kofman a way of making her unmanageably aporetic past manageable.[9] By having the term *mar* slide along a provocative chain of puns in modern French, Kofman relates how her readings about the medieval term combined with her fear about a nighttime flight she would soon take on a Tuesday (*mar-di*). This produced a night-*mare*, a *cauche-mar*, in which the rue *Mar*-cadet appears, a flashpoint of Kofman's traumatic departure from her childhood home:

> I am in a room from my childhood, with my mother, my brothers and sisters, at night. A bird enters, a kind of bat with a human head, pronouncing in a loud voice: 'Woe [*malheur*] unto you! Woe unto you!'
>
> My mother and I, terrorized, run away. We are in tears in the rue Marcadet; we know we are in great danger and fear death. I awaken very anxious. (CSS, 108–9/NM, 253)[10]

As she interprets the meaning of this frightening apparition (CSS, 109–10), Kofman offers a condensed summary of events later told in *Rue Ordener, Rue Labat*. *Mar*, she writes, 'induced the return of an entire buried past, belonging to an entirely other age, to [her] middle ages' (CSS, 108/NM, 253).[11]

Although Kofman's use of puns involving *mar* has been acknowledged in the critical literature, medieval subject matter itself has not yet been considered as a means of deepening our understanding of this enigmatic essay.[12] This is surprising, given the extent to which the use of medieval language seems to have enabled the text's remarkable cascade of philosophical, autobiographical and literary meanings — a synthesis which arguably defines Kofman's legacy as a thinker, but which had not yet appeared in such a form.[13] Even when considered in the context of a broader French poststructuralist vogue for the medieval (Lacan, for example, frequently cited medieval literature and philosophy), there is nothing that compares to the personal, affective charge of this essay, nor the directness of Kofman's philological engagement with medieval language in an untranslated form.[14] Despite her claim to be 'Neither a linguist nor a medievalist' (CSS, 108/NM, 253), the book by Cerquiglini in which Kofman encountered *mar* contains over 400 untranslated citations in Old French; it could rightly be characterized as a technical manual addressed to specialists in medieval linguistics, specifically. What she drew from it could only have been the fruit of a close critical engagement.

In this essay, I propose to take Kofman's meaning *à la lettre* when she writes that *mar* 'induced the return' of '[her] middle ages', thereby implying that medieval material and her own aporetic past can be thought to occupy the same conceptual position. When Kofman mapped her own traumatic experience onto the Middle Ages and used an untranslatable medieval word to access it, I believe that she was working from an understanding of the affective register of the Middle Ages which others have also posited when working at the juncture of psychoanalysis and the medieval. The French medievalist Jean-Charles Huchet, for example, has argued that medieval and psychoanalytic meanings intersect in the 'very heart of suffering'; he advocated for what he called a 'literary clinic', a sort of anti-interpretive practice in which scholars working at this intersection should seek to tease out 'a meaning that remains pending/suffering [*en souffrance*] in the text' (Huchet plays with an untranslatable blending of these meanings), rather than imposing the equivalent of a hasty diagnosis.[15] By following the threads that lead from the medieval term *mar* to unexplored aspects of Kofman's essay (and indeed to the medieval era itself), I shall argue that the whole of 'Nightmare' can be found to function as a literary clinic in Huchet's sense. Through two figures in particular — the bat from the nightmare and Lilith — conceptual ties to the Middle Ages are mapped onto the points of the most acute, aporetic suffering animating the essay (and vice versa), opening new avenues by which the nightmare can be interpreted in the process.

Echoes of the Bat

In her important analysis of Kofman's nightmare, F. K. Clementi observed that the bat with a human head unmistakably recalls a personal dream recounted by Freud in *The Interpretation of Dreams*, in which a young Sigmund beholds '[his] beloved mother (. . .) being carried into the room by two (or three) people with birds' beaks and laid upon the bed'.[16] Freud would later return to this dream in his reading of Leonardo da Vinci's own bird dream, which Kofman has repeatedly explored.[17]

I propose to take this line of thinking a step further by considering the whole of Kofman's nightmare as a referential space, one in which we can witness the link Kofman posits between the Middle Ages and her own personal points of suffering playing itself out in practice. Kofman herself points in this direction. Just as the medieval lexeme *mar* conjures 'an essentially dramatic fate' (CSS, 107/NM, 252; see PM, 129), her nightmare possesses literary qualities: she calls it 'a dream (…) — an epic dream? — a dreadful night-*mare*'; it is 'a text ruled by a singular code, an entirely personal syntax and grammar' (CSS, 108/NM, 253), echoing the earlier description of *mar* itself as 'the extremely coded sign of a discourse' (CSS, 105/NM, 252).

What might this approach reveal about the meaning of the bat with a human head, a figure in the dream-text whose hybridity mirrors *mar*'s dual status as both *poros* and *aporia*? One of the difficulties in parsing the conclusion to *Comment s'en sortir?* is that Kofman offers two different potential interpretations of her dream, without explicitly weighing in on which of the two should be taken as definitive.[18] In the first interpretation, Kofman reads the bat as a figure that brings paradoxical relief. By forcing her and her mother to flee, the bat shifts the context of the dream to 1943, where Kofman is able to see that she *survived* her efforts to hide from Nazi roundups, even when she 'feared the worst' (CSS, 110/NM, 254); the upcoming flight certainly posed no greater threat than what she had overcome in the past. The bat's hybridity therefore reflects the condensation of meanings coming from two different directions: first, the 'night flight' which Kofman feared (represented by the part that appeared as an anatomical bat); second, the man from the Kommandantur, represented by the human face uttering the warning. However, Kofman's second interpretation is different: in the concluding 'post-scriptum', she subsequently holds the bat to condense 'in one image' the man from the Kommandantur with the figure of 'the old sorceress *Maredewitch*', which her biological mother regularly used to frighten her (CSS, 111–12/NM, 254).

Despite their divergences, these interpretations have two important elements in common: they posit the bat with a human head as a figure central to the meaning of the nightmare, and they stress the bat's ability in the dream-work to condense two different meanings into one form. With its uncanny combination of bird-like wings and a resemblance to rodents, the bat does not seem to be a random choice of animal to illustrate this kind of condensation. If the nightmare functions as a referential space, as I argue, then it becomes possible to ask a new question: where might Kofman have encountered bats, engaged with their symbolic meaning as hybrid forms?

Among the few literary works listed as influences in Kofman's autobiography, the famous *Fables* of Jean de La Fontaine stand out: they appear on three separate occasions in the short text.[19] The first memory seems to be a happy one, albeit tinged with her attempts to cope under forced exile: the narrator would recite *The Cockerel, the Cat, and the Little Mouse* to amuse her classmates (RO, 24/30). The second reference is more sinister: the narrator receives an illustrated copy of *The Cricket and the Ant* as a paradoxical 'reward' given to her in a school competition intended to enforce Pétain's politics of 'work, family, and fatherland', from which she was in fact excluded (RO, 45/55–6). The third is ambivalent, as Mémé compels the narrator to memorize *The Cat, the Weasel, and the Little Rabbit* (RO, 47/58).

In light of this, it seems safe to posit that Kofman would also have encountered another of the collection's better-known fables, *The Bat and the Two Weasels*, which explicitly asserts that the bat has two different essences that overlap within the frame of a single body. La Fontaine's fable tells of a bat who was trapped by a weasel with a hatred of mice; thinking quickly, the bat responds that she is in fact a bird, offering her wings as evidence:

> Me, a mouse! Wicked ones have told you this news:
> Thanks to the Author of the universe,
> I am a Bird: look at my wings.[20]

Later, the hapless bat finds herself in the same situation again, only this time with a weasel who hates *birds*; now the bat asserts that she cannot be a bird, because *plumage* makes the bird: 'What makes a bird? It's the plumage. I am a Mouse: long live the Rats' (see F, 76). Because of her quick thinking and the way in which the ambivalent composition of her body allows for either thesis to be sustained, the bat escapes both times. In the end, the moral intervenes to connect the bat to opportunistic people (the bat falls among those who are 'of shifting allegiance [*d'écharpe changeants*]', see F, 76), but with a measure of ironic distance, also potentially to the 'wise': 'A wise person says, according to the circumstance [*selon les gens*]: Long live the King, long live the League' (see F, 76).[21]

Because of Kofman's avid reading of La Fontaine, as well as the way in which she associates the dreaming of a hybrid bat with a recollection from her own life, certain parallels between La Fontaine's fable and events recounted elsewhere in Kofman's life-writing provide a significant field of resonance in the context of the dream. In particular, the fable recalls the frustrating passage of *Rue Ordener, Rue Labat* in which Kofman points out turncoats of precisely this type: she tells of a Nazi collaborator who lived in her building during the Occupation, and who proclaimed her love for the F. F. I. immediately upon the liberation of Paris (RO, 57/68).

Other aspects of the fable recall Kofman's own aporetic situation as recounted in *Rue Ordener, Rue Labat*. The two-natured bat is forced to use her rhetorical cunning to survive encounters with two predators that have incompatible but equally threatening expectations. This double-bind of two predatory weasels recalls the overall narrative structure of Kofman's autobiography: one mother-figure (Mémé) embodies the paradoxes of survival under Nazi Occupation, whereas the other mother-figure (the biological one) is innocent of Nazi violence but guilty of relentless physical and emotional abuse. Each weasel-mother compels the narrator to give them what they want at different times in order to win their affections, forcing the young girl constantly to compromise her own identity — just as the bat does — in order to appease the two mothers' capricious and incompatible symbolic demands.

In an uncanny bearing-out of Kofman's suggestion that medieval material and her own suffering occupy the same conceptual place in 'Nightmare', the actual Middle Ages appear in the margins of this drama of rival identities. Prior to the medieval era, there was no strong association between bats and hybridity or duality in the West; the animal had been perceived mainly as diabolical or impure (see Leviticus 11:19; Deuteronomy 14:18). This changed with the parallel rise to popularity of two extremely similar beast fables, the most influential of the two being a Latin fable in which a bat opportunistically attempts to switch sides in a war between the beasts and the birds, since its anatomy permits it to make a case for either identity.[22] This fable had already profoundly influenced standard animal symbolism in the West by the time La Fontaine selected a parallel fable in Greek recounting similar events (the Bat and the Two Weasels).[23]

It is unlikely that Kofman was aware of the resonance linking La Fontaine's fable to the medieval notion of the bat's hybridity. However, I do not think it purely coincidental that an essay titled 'At the Margins of Medieval Studies' and overwhelmingly dedicated to the analysis of a medieval adverb should culminate in a nightmare that prominently exhibits medieval animal symbolism. What the presence of such symbolism reveals, I think, is the richness of the structural homology that Kofman intuited between her own suffering and the various means of expressing grief and personal anguish which medieval sources have left to us. As Huchet predicted in his vision of a 'literary clinic', Kofman's own personal 'middle ages' opens onto 'a meaning that remains pending/suffering' in the margins of the dream-text, one with uncanny links to the medieval imaginary that can tell us more about the nature of her nightmare — whether they were intended or not.

'Lilith, or the Dark Mother'

Kofman concludes *Comment s'en sortir?* with a post-scriptum that returns to the meaning of her nightmare, this time with the aid of a book by Jacques Bril about Lilith, a figure interpreted as a demoness in Jewish folklore.[24] Kofman relates that three months after having the nightmare, she learned that Lilith sometimes assumes the form of a bat; still another of Lilith's forms is that of *Marewip*, which Kofman ties to a painful childhood memory in which her biological mother would lock her in a 'dark closet' with the threat that the phantom *Maredewitchalè* would come and either devour her or take her 'far away from home' (CSS, 111–12/NM, 254). Kofman makes this connection by citing the root *mare* that both *Marewip* and *Maredewitchalè* 'probably' share (CSS, 111/NM, 254).[25] She notes that this root can also be found in the French term 'nightmare' (*cauchemar*), implicitly tying the entire thread of meanings that implicate Lilith back to the medieval adverb *mar* which had spurred her dream in the first place.

Although the post-scriptum is short, it raises a number of intriguing questions about the preceding dream and its proper interpretation. Kofman explicitly states that the chain of associations leading from *mar* to the Maredewitch (with Lilith positioned as the intermediary term in the chain) was produced based on knowledge acquired '[t]hree months after having this nightmare' while reading a book about Lilith by Jacques Bril. Logically, then, this knowledge of forms taken by Lilith and the etymological resonance of the word *Marewip* cannot have been present at the time of the nightmare. Acknowledging as much, Kofman concedes that when she imagined the *Maredewitchalè* as a girl, she did not imagine the form of a bat (which would provide the link to Lilith), but rather 'a very old woman' (CSS, 112/NM, 254). One nonetheless senses that Kofman ascribes meaning to the discovery *après-coup* that

Lilith took the form of the bat, since this discovery provides the needed connection between the nightmare and *Marewip* (a figure also discussed in Bril's book).[26]

The way in which Kofman appears to resolve this temporal dilemma raises still further questions. Kofman cites a distinction taken up by Freud in *Studies on Hysteria* between the 'official' knowledge of the conscious mind and the 'unofficial' (*officieux*) knowledge retained by the unconscious (CSS, 112/NM, 254). Freud first marked a distinction between these two kinds of knowledge when he noticed that his patient Frau Cäcilie M. seemed to predict the future of her own pathology: if she said, 'It's a long time since I've been frightened of witches at night', the analyst knew that 'a severe onset of her fear of witches' would promptly follow.[27] Recalling that Kofman characterizes the Maredewitch as a 'witch' (*sorcière*), it seems unlikely that her unstated choice to cite a passage in Freud dealing with the nighttime fear of witches was coincidental.[28] Kofman thus seems to suggest that her subsequent discovery about Lilith's tie to the *Maredewitchalè* is a valid element in the interpretation of the dream's meaning, because it merely confirmed something she knew about in advance (as Frau Cäcilie M. knew of her coming fear of witches). But what, exactly, did she know?

F. K. Clementi has convincingly argued that Kofman's reference to 'unofficial' knowledge could be taken to mean that a young Kofman unconsciously recognized the threat posed by Mémé (and indeed her own biological mother) by picturing *Maredewitchalè* as an old woman; this figure embodies 'the pull of two mothers', echoing the frighteningly ambivalent 'pre-oedipal mother' recognizable in Freud's own nightmare (NNM, 90).[29] I would add that the text of the post-scriptum is also structured ambiguously enough to allow the notion of 'unofficial' knowledge to connect back up to Lilith and the discovery *après-coup* of her connection to bats and the frightening figure of the 'nocturnal spirit' (CSS, 111/NM, 254). This would mean that Kofman already unconsciously, 'unofficially' knew enough about Lilith to make the jump from the bat to the night phantom without having needed to read Bril's book. Kofman, after all, had a well-established interest in the *Maredewitchalè*, and the very choice to read Bril's book suggests a prior interest in its folkloric resonance. If Kofman was ever aware that the Hebrew (לִילִית *lilít*) is often rendered as 'owl' or another nocturnal animal in translations of Isaiah 34:14, this too would be sufficient to provide the connection.

For further clues about Lilith's relevance to the interpretation of the dream, we can follow the medieval traces at the margins of Kofman's essay. The first resonance to consider is the one linking Lilith to the bat's symbolic hybridity. Although Kofman does not quote Bril directly or cite this particular aspect of his account, the passage on *Marewip* ('women of the sea') that she cites from his book bears unmistakable resemblance to the dreamt bat's turncoat hybridity: 'although aquatic, they [the *Marewip*] can fly through the air thanks to a magical plumage, but they can also leave [this plumage] in the way one takes off an article of clothing, and they then have the appearance of ordinary women' (LMO, 100). Lilith's ties to the bat are further strengthened by the formula that they seem to share: in the dream-text, the bat says, 'Woe unto you [*malheur à vous*]' (CSS, 108/NM, 253); in his book, Bril warns that 'In the night, woe to the man [*malheur à l'homme*] onto whom Lilith's desire is directed' (LMO, 66).

A more concrete trace of the medieval can help further clarify Lilith's importance, this time with respect to the semantic field of ambivalent mothers uncovered by Clementi's analysis. In Bril's book, one of the most important legends associated with Lilith is noted to have originated in the Middle Ages. The tale in question comes from the 'Alphabet of Ben Sira', a key text in medieval rabbinic circles as a source of both entertainment and knowledge.[30] The work is constructed as a series of questions asked to Ben Sira by King Nebuchadnezzar. In response to the fifth question, Ben Sira tells of how God created Lilith as an initial companion for Adam, using earth rather than Adam's rib as would later be done in the case of Eve. This troubling element of equality meant that their respective notions of how sex acts should express gender hierarchy were incompatible: Lilith refused to lie below Adam, causing her to fly away into the air (like a bat). Punished by God, she is doomed to see her own children die by the hundreds, and in retaliation seeks to harm human infants (ABS, 183). Kofman's awareness of this medieval legend surrounding Lilith, as discussed in Bril's book, is evidenced by her characterization of Lilith as 'the first seductive and devouring Eve' (CSS, 111/NM, 254).[31]

Just prior in Bril's book, we learn that Lilith has sometimes been identified by Kabbalists as one of the two women in the Judgement of Solomon narrative (1 Kings 3:16–28), each claiming to be a child's rightful mother. What might come as a surprise, given the extent of Lilith's negative connotation as a demoness in Jewish folklore, is that some Kabbalists have identified Lilith as the 'good mother', the one whom Solomon identifies as the true mother by her reaction of compassion for the child about to be split in two (LMO, 68). The result, in Bril's formulation, is that Lilith is 'contradictory'; she is 'at once sinister and beneficial' (LMO, 201).

Both of these aspects of Lilith's lore are likely to have intrigued Kofman. As Bril notes, the tale in which Lilith refuses to submit to Adam constitutes a 'categorical affirmation by woman of the domestic equality of the sexes' (LMO, 124–5) — one which leads Lilith to be punished as a mother, specifically. The two mothers of the Judgement of Solomon, for their part, have obvious resonance in the context of events recounted in Kofman's life-writing.[32]

When these threads are considered together, Lilith can be recognized as an ambivalent mother-figure in Kofman's essay, one whose role in condensing maternal meanings hides in plain sight as the title of Bril's book: *Lilith, ou la mère obscure* (Lilith, or the Dark Mother). As to whether Lilith should be thought to correlate to Mémé or to Kofman's biological mother, I believe the very point is that she cannot be reduced to either. Frightening and yet attractive, cruel and yet compassionate, the Lilith conveyed by Bril's book unmistakably evokes Mémé; on the other hand, Kofman's biological mother is recognizable in the vision of Lilith as a punishing mother, but one who was herself unjustly punished (for asserting her own equality to Adam, or her right to remain the parent of her own daughter).

Like the untranslatable *mar* which is both *aporia* and *poros*, like the bat that is both beast and bird, human and animal, Lilith functions in Kofman's essay as 'a meaning that remains pending/suffering' — a point at which the personal suffering of Kofman's 'middle ages' and the Middle Ages meet on paper, giving shape to trauma without resolving it.

Conclusion: Does It Come Back Alive?

'The particle *mar*, that segment of a vanished language, induced the return of an entire buried past, belonging to an entirely other age, to my middle ages' (CSS, 108/NM, 253). Close readers of Kofman will recognize in the term 'buried', and particularly in the notion of a buried past, a rich thread that runs through the whole of her career. As early as her first book, *The Childhood of Art*, Kofman took an interest in Freud's tendency to compare the uncovering of unconscious material to the work of an archaeologist scrutinizing ruins and discovering hidden artefacts (CA, 33, 64–5, 68–70).[33] Kofman would return to the metaphor of a buried past in *Un métier impossible* (An Impossible Profession), albeit with a new clarification about the limits of the metaphor: that which becomes psychically 'buried' through repression is never dead in the manner of an old ruin, but rather *alive* and actively trying to be found (U, 80). This notion of meanings buried alive bears painful echoes of the fate of Kofman's own father, the rabbi Bereck Kofman, himself 'buried alive' (RO, 10/16) at Auschwitz.

In a passage selected by Kofman for inclusion in the chapter 'Nightmare', the medievalist Cerquiglini confidently claims that by analysing *mar*, one can make it come back alive: 'A syntax thought to be inert rises up alive, from the heart of alterity, not animated by our feelings but by the respect, and by the meticulous examination of that which founds its difference' (quoted in CSS, 105/NM, 252). This thread links us back into the Greek term *aporia*, which Kofman shows (via Plato) to be connoted with death by drowning, and also (via Blanchot) to constitute a radically ungraspable alterity that resists straightforward conceptualization (CSS, 97–8/BA, 41). To the extent that it can come back alive from within the heart of alterity, *mar* reads like a *poros*, a way out from the aporia. Kofman, however, deconstructs Cerquiglini's rhetoric on this point: isn't he really saying that death and marginal status (*marginalité*) are the same, that one can fight both at once through the 'fantastic (. . .) diabolical pleasure of bringing the dead person to life' (CSS, 106/NM, 252)?[34] Her subtle pessimism about the capacity to bring anything fully back to life, even through efforts like Cerquiglini's, manifests in her continued use of 'the dead person' to describe that which has ostensibly been reanimated.

Two beings at the margin between life and death, between reality and unreality, between autobiography and philosophy, surged forth from Kofman's use of *mar*: Lilith and a hybrid bat. The close study of these figures and their representations in Kofman's text leads us down a trail to some of her most acute points of suffering, the still-living contents of her 'buried past', her own 'middle ages'.

We shall never fully pin down the 'ça' of Kofman's thinking, reduce it to a neat diagnosis, a comfortable reference, a coherent genre. Neither wholly autobiographical nor wholly philosophical, Kofman's thought is a bat-thought, cunningly escaping our attempts to trap it. A bat but a human, Lilith but a mother, its alterity always comes back.

NOTES

1 Sarah Kofman, '"My Life" and Psychoanalysis', translated by Georgia Albert, in *Selected Writings*, edited by Thomas Albrecht, with Georgia Albert and Elizabeth Rottenberg (Stanford, CA: Stanford University Press, 2007), 250–1.

2 Sarah Kofman, 'Tomb for a Proper Name' and 'Damned Food', translated by Frances Bartowski and Georgia Albert, in *Selected Writings*, 247–8 and 248–9, hereafter TP and DF, respectively.

3 I omit from this list a fragmentary dream narrative not published by Kofman during her lifetime, but recently discovered in her archive: Sarah Kofman, 'La Mort Blanche', *Fusées* 16 (2009), 7. On this text, see Isabelle Ullern, 'La philosophie "biographée" selon Sarah Kofman', *L'Atelier du centre de recherches historiques [en ligne]* 21 (2019), http://journals.openedition.org/acrh/9933, hereafter LP.

4 Sarah Kofman, *Comment s'en sortir?* (Paris: Galilée, 1983), hereafter CSS. (Editor's note: See 'Beyond Aporia?', translated by David Macey, in *Post-structuralist Classics*, edited by Andrew Benjamin (London and New York: Routledge, 1988), 7–44, hereafter BA.) On the unique staging of philosophy and autobiography together within *Comment s'en sortir?*, see Rachel Rosenblum, 'And Till the Ghastly Tale is Told: Sarah Kofman — Primo Levi: Survivors of the Shoah and the Dangers of Testimony', translated by Saskia Brown, *European Judaism: A Journal for the New Europe* 33:2 (2000), 92–4, hereafter AG. See also LP, 12 (para. 7), and Rachel Rosenblum, 'Distancing Emotion: Surviving the Account of Catastrophe', *Passions in Context* 2:1 (2011), 136–8.

5 See the allusion to the story of Arion and the Dolphin in *Republic* 453d–e, discussed in CSS, 24–5/BA, 11–12. Translations of CSS are my own for all sections except the final chapter, which I quote from Sarah Kofman, 'Nightmare: At the Margins of Medieval Studies', translated by Frances Bartkowski, in *Selected Writings*, 251–4, hereafter NM.

6 On this point, see the moving analysis offered by Rosenblum in AG, 94.

7 Bernard Cerquiglini, *La Parole médiévale: discours, syntaxe, texte* (Paris: Minuit, 1981), hereafter PM.

8 Cerquiglini finds this explanation unsatisfying (PM, 135). For an account of the many etymological explanations of this lexeme, see W. von Wartburg, CNRS, and ATILF, *Französisches Etymologisches Wörterbuch*, 25 volumes (Bonn: Schröder, 1922–2002), volume IV, 476.

9 The point is taken up in Kathryn Robson, 'Bodily Detours: Sarah Kofman's Narratives of Childhood Trauma', *The Modern Language Review* 99:3 (2004), 620, hereafter BD.

10 See Sarah Kofman, *Rue Ordener, Rue Labat*, translated by Ann Smock (Lincoln, NE: University of Nebraska Press, 1996), 31; Sarah Kofman, *Rue Ordener, rue Labat* (Paris: Galilée, 1994), 40, hereafter RO; page numbers are to the English-language edition followed by the French-language edition. See also AG, 93.

11 I adapt Bartowski's otherwise excellent translation at this point in order to illustrate the connection to the medieval: Bartowski employs 'my dark ages', whereas the original French has the more neutral 'mon moyen âge'. I preserve Kofman's choice not to capitalize the term, where elsewhere she does (CSS, 107).

12 See F. K. Clementi, 'Nightbirds, Nightmares and the Mothers' Smile: Art and Psychoanalysis in Sarah Kofman's Life-Writing', *Women in French Studies* 19 (2011), 78–9, hereafter NNM. See also Tina Chanter, 'Eating Words: Antigone as Kofman's Proper Name', in *Enigmas: Essays on Sarah Kofman*, ed. Penelope Deutscher and Kelly Oliver (Ithaca, NY: Cornell University Press, 1999), 189–202 (194), hereafter EWA.

13 Kofman herself predicts this legacy in Sarah Kofman and Alice Jardine, 'An Interview', translated by Janice Orion, *New Political Science* 15:3–4 (n.d.), 28.

14 For a detailed exposition of this tendency in Lacan, see Erin Felicia Labbie, *Lacan's Medievalism* (Minneapolis, MN: University of Minnesota Press, 2006).

15 Jean-Charles Huchet, *Littérature médiévale et psychanalyse: pour une clinique littéraire* (Paris: Presses universitaires de France, 1990), 22–4.

16 Sigmund Freud, *The Standard Edition of the Complete Psychological Works of Sigmund Freud*, translated by James Strachey, volume V (London: Hogarth Press, 1953), 583.

17 See, for example, Sarah Kofman, *The Childhood of Art* (New York: Columbia University Press, 1988), 61, hereafter CA.

18 See also EWA.

19 Jean de La Fontaine, *Œuvres complètes I: Fables, contes et nouvelles*, edited by Jean-Pierre Collinet (Paris: Gallimard, 1991), hereafter F.

20 See F, 75. Translations from La Fontaine are mine unless indicated otherwise.

21 The question of to what extent La Fontaine meant for us to take this epimythium at its word is taken up by Jean-Pierre Collinet in F, 1082n. 75.

22 See Jean Batany, '"The Marginal Beast": la chauve-souris des fables et l'ambiguïté d'un statut', *Reinardus* 14 (2001), 6–7, 12, and J. Leclercq-Marx, 'Un animal très ambigu', *Reinardus* 28:1 (2016), 114.

23 On La Fontaine and the texts contained in his Renaissance source 'Nevelet', see F, 1032.

24 Jacques Bril, *Lilith, ou la mère obscure* (Paris: Payot, 1984), hereafter LMO.

25 My translation of the French 'sans doute' differs from Bartowski, who renders it as 'undoubtedly' here.

26 LMO, 100. See BD, 620.

27 Sigmund Freud, *The Standard Edition of the Complete Psychological Works of Sigmund Freud,* translated by James Strachey, volume II (London: Hogarth Press, 1955), 76n. 1.

28 See Sarah Kofman's treatment of the same passage in *Un métier impossible: lecture de 'Constructions en analyse'* (Paris: Galilée, 1983), 45–7, where the fear of witches is mentioned, hereafter U.

29 On the pre-oedipal mother, Clementi quotes from Sara van den Berg, 'Reading the Object: Freud's Dreams', *PSYART: A Hyperlink Journal for the Psychological Study of the Arts* (1997), article 970501.

30 On the Alphabet of Ben Sira, see LMO, 70–2 and 124–5. For the Alphabet's medieval dating ('possibly as early as the eighth century'), see 'The Alphabet of Ben Sira' in *Rabbinic Fantasies: Imaginative Narratives from Classical Hebrew Literature,* translated by Norman Bronznick, David Stern and Mark Jay Mirsky, edited by David Stern and Mark Jay Mirsky (New Haven, CT: Yale University Press, 1990), 167, hereafter ABS. On the 'respectability' of the Alphabet, see ABS, 168.

31 Editor's note: See also Sarah Kofman, *The Enigma of Woman,* translated by Catherine Porter (Ithaca, NY: Cornell University Press, 1985), 224–5.

32 The resonance between the Judgement of Solomon narrative and events recounted in Kofman's life-writing has been remarked elsewhere. F. K. Clementi, for example, has linked the Judgement of Solomon to the F. F. I. trial scene in which the narrator of *Rue Ordener, Rue Labat* testifies against her biological mother (NNM, 73).

33 It is worth noting that in this first monograph, Kofman invokes the action of 'unearthing the past as if it existed elsewhere than its traces' as an example of what Freud does *not* endorse as a method of artistic interpretation. See CA, 64–5.

34 On Kofman's characterization of Cerquiglini as making the unmanageable 'terrible force' of *mar* into a manageable 'mechanical toy' (CSS 106–7), see EWA, 194.

Freud's Jewish Jokes: The Case of *Jokes and Their Relation to the Unconscious*

ELIZABETH ROTTENBERG

Introduction: Putting Freud on the Couch

What is at play in play? What does it mean to take play seriously? Or, in the case of Sigmund Freud, what does it means to take jokes seriously? In this essay I will argue that a contemporary reading of Freud's *Joke* Book provides us with one of the most serious and playful responses to these questions. But first I will go out on a limb: I will bet the house that 'Sarah Kofman' is not the first name that springs to mind in the context of play — certainly not if you think of play as levity and mirth. Although she may have 'laughed a lot', as Jacques Derrida tells us, or 'loved to joke', as she herself confesses, Sarah Kofman was not, at least in my experience, what you would call a playful person.[1] And yet, I would argue, her insistence on play — indeed her insistence on her own playfulness or 'humour' (*esprit de jeu*) (RO, 96/81) at the end of what is perhaps her least playful, most disturbing book, *Rue Ordener, rue Labat*, published shortly before her suicide in 1994 — should not be taken lightly. For Kofman is also a thinker who takes play, the force and significance of play, in particular in Freud's work, seriously. Whether it is aesthetic play (*L'Enfance de l'art* (1970)), witticisms and jokes (*Pourquoi rit-on?* (1986)), speculative play (*'Il n'y a que le premier pas qui coûte'* (1991)), or the play of analysis (*Un métier impossible* (1983)), Kofman brings out the play *in* play. In a rather Winnicottian vein, she brings out the space of indetermination in play that provides not only 'relief' — 'relief' from philosophy, as we will see in her 1986 book *Pourquoi rit-on?* (Why Do We Laugh?) — but also, fundamentally, pleasure.[2]

Paragraph 44.1 (2021): 103–116
DOI: 10.3366/para.2021.0357

www.euppublishing.com/para

For it is pleasure and also, I will suggest, a kind of *Oedipal* play that lead Kofman to analyse Freud's 1905 book *Jokes and Their Relation to the Unconscious*, that is, to put it (and therefore him) on the couch.[3]

Why so Defensive?

Imagine the scene: not Plato reaching over the back of a chair to put his finger in Socrates' back but a philosopher sitting back in her chair in order to put the father of psychoanalysis back on the couch. What prompts the philosopher to play the analyst (and I do not mean this as a euphemism; Kofman is not 'playing analyst' the way one 'plays doctor'; no one plays the analyst more seriously than Sarah Kofman) is the initial presentation of Freud's book. From the outset, *d'entrée de jeu*, Kofman is struck by this appearance:

> *Jokes and Their Relation to the Unconscious* is, by all appearances, Freud's most philosophical work. Veritable *corpus* having both head and legs, divided in the most Hegelian way into three parts — an analytic, a synthetic, and a theoretic part — it sets out, in its very introduction, to gather into living tissue earlier reflections on the subject, scattered here and there, in order to organize them into a system. Freud is looking to combine 'into an organic whole' what he calls, alluding to the Latin poet Horace, the *disjecta membra* in order to give them life, form, meaning.[4]

Three parts, a systematic effort to organize, synthesize, unify what had been scattered here and there by his predecessors: Kofman calls attention to what would appear to be Freud's most philosophical book.

Yet, as is well known, no one in the history of psychoanalysis was more ambivalent about philosophy than Freud. No one was more fascinated and repelled by philosophical abstractions than the father of psychoanalysis; no one was more eager to propound the idea of a 'similarity and (. . .) kinship'[5] between the delusions of paranoiacs and the 'artificially constructed systems' of philosophers (SE XIX, 217). Thus, if Kofman raises an eyebrow, it is because she takes Freud's philosophical penchant with a grain of — analytic — salt; the philosophical appearance of the *Joke* Book would be but its 'manifest content'. What Kofman is telling us, if I can put it this way, is that we should take Freud literally but not seriously. After all, *Jokes and Their Relation to the Unconscious* literally gives the appearance of a philosophical work. It is a theory of jokes complete with a middle and extremities. But if we take this appearance too seriously, if we *mis*take the 'manifest content' for the latent thought, we lose the play of Kofman's analytic play.

For Kofman is too Freudian not to recognize a symptom when she sees one. When the Analyst of analysts becomes defensively philosophical, the well-analysed philosopher puts the analyst on the couch. And, in many ways, *Pourquoi rit-on?* reads like a 'case study':

> In the *Joke* Book, more than anywhere else, Freud multiplies his defence systems. The book's composition in three parts could be seen as one of these systems, as well as his desire to unify and synthesize the *membra disjecta* [sic] of his predecessors and, in this way, to establish his pre-eminence over them. (PRO, 61)

What is more, like any good case study, *Pourquoi rit-on?* regales us with details of the early history of the *Joke* Book. There is evidence, notes Kofman, of Freud's early interest in jokes: on 22 June 1897, for example, he confesses to Wilhelm Fliess that he has been putting together 'a collection of Jewish anecdotes of deep significance'.[6] And then, a few months later, on 21 September 1897, he describes a Jewish joke as coming 'from my collection' (CL, 266). Far more compelling, on the other hand — and providing grist for the analytic mill — are Freud's avowed 'personal motives' (SE VIII, 15) and 'subjective reason[s]' (SE VIII, 173) for taking on the subject of jokes. Indeed, it would seem that the writing of *Jokes and Their Relation to the Unconscious* was precipitated by what could only be called an 'Oedipal conflict'. What happened was this: when reading the proofs of *The Interpretation of Dreams* in the autumn of 1899, Fliess complained to Freud that the dreams were too full of jokes. The dreamer, Fliess protested, was 'too ingenious and amusing [too witty, too jokey: *zu witzig*]' (SE IV, 297n. 1/GW II/III, 393n. 1).

Freud was upset by the criticism. We know this from his response to Fliess, which is textbook — even jokebook — defensive. In the wake of Fliess's criticism, Freud will not only find it necessary to explain the kinship between the technique of jokes and dream-work; he will not only draw a clear dividing line between the wisecracking dreamer, on the one hand, and the poker-faced interpreter, on the other. He will also insist, almost comically, long before the Coen brothers' film, that he, Freud, is 'a serious man'. Both in a letter to Fliess and in a footnote to *The Interpretation of Dreams*, Freud will claim that he is but *unwittingly witty*. I will quote his letter to Fliess, dated 11 September 1899:

> It is certainly true that the dreamer is too witty (*zu witzig*), but it is neither my fault nor does it contain a reproach. All dreamers are equally insufferably witty

(*unausstehlich witzig*), and they need to be because they are under pressure and the direct route is barred to them (. . .). If you deem it necessary, I shall insert a remark to that effect somewhere. (CL, 371)

Freud will add this remark to *The Interpretation of Dreams*:

The first reader and critic of this book (. . .) objected that 'the dreamer often seems to be too witty (*zu witzig*).' This is quite true so long as it refers only to the dreamer; it would only be a reproach if it were to be extended to the dream-interpreter. In waking reality I have little claim to be regarded as a wit. If my dreams seem witty (*witzig*), that is not on my account, but on account of the particular psychological conditions under which dreams are constructed (. . .). A dream becomes witty (*witzig*) because the direct and easiest pathway to the expression of its thoughts is barred; it is forced into being so. The reader can convince himself that my patients' dreams seem at least as full of jokes and puns as my own, or even fuller. (SE IV, 297–8n. 1/GW II/III, 393–4n. 1)

'I'm not a funny guy', Freud is saying. 'Seriously, it's only my dreams that are funny and that has nothing to do with me, that has only to do with the technical methods of dream-work. And if you think *my* dreams are funny, you should hear the dreams of my patients — they're *hysterical*!'

Joking aside, however, there is clear and convincing evidence of the defensive nature of the *Joke* Book: Freud is obviously stung into action by Fliess's criticism. Considering that one of the principal purposes of *The Interpretation of Dreams* is to hail the interpretation of dreams as '*the royal road to a knowledge of the unconscious*' (SE V, 608), it must have felt like a royal betrayal to see the dreamer reduced to a vulgar jester. Which is why Kofman does not mince words when she summarizes the book's early history: 'It is to Fliess, the accusing spiritual father (. . .) that Freud addresses his justificatory discourse. And it is to Fliess that he should have dedicated this self-defensive text in which he repeats the murder of the father' (PRO, 17).

Jewish Jokes

Kofman is making a rather radical claim here: '[Freud] repeats the murder of the father' (PRO, 17). Not only, that is, does Kofman read the *Joke* Book as Freud's attempt to sever the ties that bind him to Fliess, 'the accusing spiritual father' (PRO, 17); she also reads it — in a way that is far more fundamental and far-reaching — as Freud's attempt to sever the ties that bind him 'to his actual father', that is to say, 'to *his Jewish heritage*' (PRO, 26). Indeed, and this will be the central claim of Kofman's book, Freud's ambivalent relation to his Jewish heritage is reflected in his ambivalent relation to Jewish jokes in *Jokes and Their Relation to the Unconscious.* In other words, as Kofman makes clear, *Pourquoi rit-on?* is a book that 'addresses the Jewish problem by means of the joke' (SKJD, 278n. 305). Ambivalence, however, is a complication. In this case, it means that Freud's relation to Jewish jokes will be characterized by contradictory attitudes: on the one hand, rejection of, but, on the other hand, affection for, even pleasure in, what might be called *Yiddishkeit.*

I will begin with Freud's delight in *Yiddishkeit.* It so happens that *Jokes and Their Relation to the Unconscious* is a treasury of Jewish jokes. Approximately 13% of the 'nearly two hundred jokes, anecdotes, puns, witticisms, and riddles' (JSF, 5) are Jewish insofar as they focus on the stock characters of Jewish folklore and literature: there are jokes about the *Schnorrer*, the Jewish beggar, and his denial of what is otherwise an obvious indebtedness; there are jokes about the *Schadchen*, the Jewish marriage broker, who tries to convince the prospective bridegroom of the attractiveness of his match but often reveals more than he should; there are jokes about the *Ostjuden*, the Eastern European Jews, whose cleanliness, manners and comportment do not measure up to those of the *Westjuden* in fin-de-siècle Vienna or Berlin; finally, there are jokes about the faulty thinking of Jewish mystics who equate fantasy with reality.

But if Freud's Jewish heritage is central to our understanding of the *Joke* Book, it is not only because Freud is Jewish.[7] It is also because, as Kofman shows, there is something exemplary, *theoretically* exemplary, about Jewish jokes. There is something about Jewish jokes that is singularly revealing. Just as there is something revealingly singular about the Jews who tell them: 'I do not know', writes Freud, 'whether there are many other instances of a people making fun to such a degree of its own character' (SE VIII, 112). Wittiness, for Freud, you might say, is the new chosenness. Thus, even the coarsest of Jewish jokes are capable of making us laugh and deserve our theoretical attention. For example, the 'bath jokes' that feature the Galician Jews' aversion to baths: 'Two Jews met in the neighbourhood of the bath-house. "Have you taken a bath?" asked one of them. "What?" asked the other in return, "is there one missing?"' (SE VIII, 49). Not only do such jokes make us laugh 'really heartily' (SE VIII, 49), says Freud, but they are also models of clarity; they help us identify joke techniques (in this case, double meaning and displacement).

On the one hand, then, Freud's *Joke* Book makes great play of Jewish jokes. It plays up 'a certain Jewish identity' (PRO, 28) and makes an example of Jewish wit. On the other hand, however, 'an altogether different gesture tends to cover over the Jewish specificity of Jewish jokes' (PRO, 28). Indeed, when it comes to Jewish jokes, Kofman argues, 'Freud precisely erases their specificity' (PRO, 30). He subsumes the Jewish singularity of Jewish jokes under the category of 'humanity in general' (SE VIII, 49). That is to say, Jewish jokes become uniquely universalizable for Freud.

Kofman points to one joke in particular. It is not an especially funny joke, but it is one that happens to appear twice in *Jokes and Their Relation to the Unconscious*, both times precisely in order to exemplify an aspect of joke technique. Here's the joke:

> An impoverished individual borrowed 25 florins from a prosperous acquaintance, with many asseverations of his necessitous circumstances. The very same day his benefactor met him again with a plate of salmon mayonnaise in front of him. The benefactor reproached him: 'What? You borrow money from me and then order yourself salmon mayonnaise? Is *that* what you've used my money for?' 'I don't understand you', replied the object of the attack; 'if I haven't any money I *can't* eat salmon mayonnaise, and if I have some money I *mustn't* eat salmon mayonnaise. Well, then, when *am* I to eat salmon mayonnaise?' (SE VIII, 49–50)

When Freud first introduces this joke, he describes it as 'the purest example' (SE VIII, 51, modified) of the technique known as 'displacement', a technique whose essence lies in transporting us from one train of thought to another. Here, the displacement is from the benefactor's reproachful question to the *Schnorrer*'s sophistical response. The *Schnorrer* (and a *Schnorrer* is a beggar or scrounger in Yiddish) 'defends himself for having spent the money lent him on a delicacy and asks, with an appearance of reason, *when* he is to eat salmon' (SE VIII, 50). But such a reply begs the question. The *Schnorrer* is not being reproached for eating salmon on any particular day. It is not a question of *when* the *Schnorrer* should eat salmon. He should not be eating salmon at all: *Schnorrers* can't be choosers. If we laugh, that is, it is because 'the impoverished *bon vivant* disregards the only possible meaning of the reproach and answers another question as if he had misunderstood the reproach' (SE VIII, 50).

But the 'Salmon Mayonnaise' joke is 'highly instructive' (SE VIII, 56) in another way as well; it is the 'model case' (SE VIII, 54) of a cynical joke. And here Kofman draws our attention to the way Freud frames and uses the joke: Freud will insist that, although the joke is obviously a Jewish one — 'It is again a Jewish joke' — nevertheless 'it is merely its setting that is Jewish, its core belongs to humanity in general' (SE VIII, 49). In other words, behind the outer shell or façade of the story, which has all the trappings of Jewish folklore (the *Schnorrer*, the salmon, the *Lachs*, which is very close to laughter in German, *Lache*), lies 'a universal moral', writes Kofman, 'human all too human: cynicism' (PRO, 31). The cynical truth is that the *Schnorrer* is right: there is nothing better than enjoyment and it does not matter how one gets it. Here, as so often, a joke 'betrays something serious' (SE VIII, 107). In the case of the *Schnorrer*, it is that 'the wishes and desires of human beings have a right to make themselves acceptable alongside of exacting and ruthless morality' (SE VIII, 110). At bottom, Freud explains, the moral of the 'Salmon Mayonnaise' joke is 'nothing other than the poet's "*Carpe diem*", which appeals to the uncertainty of life and the unfruitfulness of virtuous renunciation' (SE VIII, 109). Far from giving us something specifically Jewish, that is, the *Schnorrer*'s tale remains an epicurean story. As Kofman writes: 'By displacing the accent (. . .) from the Jew to the pagan (the epicurean, the Roman), Freud reduces the joke to a universal moral truth' (PRO, 31–2). As it turns out, this universal moral truth is also eminently translatable, from *Schnorrer* joke to Latin epigram to Italian maxim: '"*Carpe diem*"', writes Freud, 'has become a serious warning. I will gladly put off satisfaction: but do I know whether I shall still be here tomorrow? "*Di doman' non c'è certezza*"' (SE VIII, 109).

What is more, says Kofman, this universalizing tendency would be true of all the Jewish jokes in *Jokes and Their Relation to the Unconscious*; all of them, writes Kofman, 'undergo (. . .) the same reduction or elevation to the universal' (PRO, 33). Kofman points in particular to Freud's marriage-broker jokes (the *Schadchen* jokes). Such jokes, you might say, add piquancy to her claim, for it is no longer just the specificity of *Jews*, it is also the specificity of (Jewish) *women* that is erased, that is to say, reduced or elevated to the universal by the cynical moral of the joke. I shall give just one example, since all the *Schadchen* jokes tell more or less of the same story:

> The bridegroom was most disagreeably surprised when the bride was introduced to him, and drew the broker on one side and whispered his remonstrances: 'Why have you brought me her?' he asked reproachfully. 'She's ugly and old, she squints and has bad teeth and bleary eyes (. . .)' — 'You needn't lower your voice', interrupted the broker, 'she's deaf as well.' (SE VIII, 64)

Again we have a cynical joke (like gefilte fish, it would seem that cynical jokes are a Jewish specialty). In this joke, says Freud, it is really the suitor who is making himself ridiculous by reducing the woman to her physical appearance and appendages. He forgets, says Freud, that he must be prepared to marry someone who is imperfect: 'a human being [here Freud uses the neuter noun: *ein Menschenkind*] with inevitable defects' (SE VIII, 108/GW VI, 118). Thus, the disguised aggressiveness of the joke is not directed against 'the woman's more or less imperfect personality' (SE VIII, 108). Not at all: it is directed 'against everyone involved in the business of arranging a marriage: the bride and bridegroom and their parents' (SE VIII, 108); it is directed against 'institutions, people in their capacity as vehicles of institutions, dogmas of morality or religion, views of life which enjoy so much respect that objections to them can only be made under the mask of a joke' (SE VIII, 108–9). What is remarkable about these jokes, says Kofman, is that, by reducing the specificity of the Jew and of the woman to a 'universalist humanism' (PRO, 52), Freud simultaneously denies the 'castration' of the Jew and the 'castration' of the woman. What Freud is saying, Kofman claims, is that '"we are all human beings", neither Jews nor Christians, neither men nor women: the Jew is a man, the woman is a man' (PRO, 52).

In short, by reducing Jewish jokes to a universal moral truth, Freud, in a defensive, philosophical way, tries to relieve them of everything Jewish. And Jewish jokes about Jewish women seem to be a point of particular sensitivity, the point at which Freud loses his good sense (*Mutterwitz*). Analytically, of course, what this means is that Kofman is leading us to the mother lode of ambivalent feeling.

Idiomatic Play

Now, Kofman's analysis of Freud's defence systems is part of a larger analysis in which Kofman discusses Freud's fetishistic position with regard to Jews and to women. In the *Joke* Book, Kofman argues, Freud oscillates, much like a fetishist, between two irreconcilable positions: Jews and women have the phallus (veneration); Jews and women are castrated (contempt).

In this essay, however, I would like to follow a slightly different path. Instead of following Kofman's serious, conceptual critique of Freud's universalization, I will follow her language, which, as we will see, returns us to Freud's language in a new way. For there is also something playful in Kofman's language, something that allows us to complicate Freud's defensive universalization of jokes, and that is the question of idiom. Needless to say, the question of idiom will not be unrelated, in the end, to the question of women.

I would like to point to a rather untranslatable word that Kofman uses, almost in passing, on at least ten occasions in *Pourquoi rit-on?*.[8] I would argue that the word is Kofman's chosen word with which to address the question of the erasure of (Jewish) specificity. Not only is the word cathected with fresh — French — excitement, as I will suggest, but it is also philosophically *relevant* to the question of play. We have seen how Freud tries to purge Jewish jokes of everything Jewish. But in quoting Kofman's commentary, I intentionally left out the idiomatic phrase she uses to describe this gesture: 'Freud reduces the joke to a universal moral truth that no longer has anything witty or funny about it; *il ôte à cette histoire tout son sel juif* (he rids or deprives the joke of all that is Jewish in it, of its Jewish *zest*, you might say)' (PRO, 32, my emphasis). Or, a few pages later: 'Thus [Freud] forces the Jewish specificity of these jokes into the background, even when, as he himself acknowledges, their Yiddishisms are what give them their *zing* (*le jargon Yiddish en fait tout le sel*)' (PRO, 36). Or, again, when it comes to the impossibility of translating the idiom of a joke: 'a joke cannot be rendered in translation (. . .) without losing its *bite* (*sous peine d'y perdre son sel*)' (PRO, 66). Again and again, *sel* does what it says: it brings out the idiom in order to keep it in play. *Sel* is salt, the 'white crystalline substance which gives seawater its characteristic taste' (*Oxford Dictionary of English*), but it is also, by extension, both in English and in French, 'something which adds freshness or piquancy', say, to a discussion. To 'add salt to a conversation' is to add zest, zing, bite, punch (as in a punchline). *C'est ce qui fait tout le sel de l'aventure*: that's what gives the adventure its spice. But *sel* in French is also another word for wit; *la remarque ne manque pas de sel*: that's quite a *witty* remark. Indeed, here Kofman's *esprit de jeu* spices up Freud's *Mot d'esprit*: where Freud subsumes (*relève*) the Jewish singularity of Jewish jokes under the universal, Kofman brings out (*relève*) their distinctive flavour — with a pinch of salt.

In other words, Kofman brings the specificity of idiom back into play, and she does so idiomatically: it is her idiomatic *French* that brings out the *Yiddish* flavour of Freud's German text. Thus, even if Freud's conceptual argument turns the Jewish joke into an example of the universal, his language and his Yiddishisms signal something else. Now, in the final pages of her book, it so happens that Kofman analyses a Jewish joke (or 'pseudo-joke' (PRO, 187)) that not only uses (Jewish) idiom but whose punchline precisely revolves around a rather sophisticated idiomatic play (in French, German and Yiddish). And, surprise surprise — the joke also depends on a problematic relation to women.

In the case of this joke, Kofman will underscore the maternal dimension of Freud's ambivalence towards all things Jewish (in other words: he is not only murdering his father, he is also mocking his mother). Indeed, the maternal dimension of the joke is absolutely essential here. So essential, in fact, that one might go so far as to say that it is the mother of all Jewish jokes in the *Joke* Book: not only is it, literally, a Jewish joke about a Jewish woman in labour, but it is also a joke in which Freud tries not once but twice to efface its Jewish heritage. '[I]t is remarkable', writes Kofman, 'that at no point does Freud mention (...) the Jewish specificity of the story' (PRO, 196). Neither in the first moment when the anecdote is deemed a 'successful joke' (SE VIII, 81) and conveys a universal moral truth. Nor in the second moment when Freud downgrades the joke to an example of 'comic unmasking' (SE VIII, 202) that serves to ridicule the impostor, here the Jewish parvenue. So, here is the 'pseudo-joke' (and I have modified Strachey's translation for reasons that will become clear in a moment):

> The doctor, who had been asked to look after the Baroness at her confinement, pronounced that the moment had not come, and suggested to the Baron that in the meantime they should have a game of cards in the next room [in other words: the woman is labouring and the men are playing cards]. After a while a cry of pain from the Baroness struck the ears of the two men: '*Ah, mon Dieu que je souffre!*' Her husband sprang up, but the doctor signed to him to sit down: 'It's nothing. Let's go on with the game!' A little later there were again sounds from the pregnant woman: '*Mein Gott, mein Gott, was für Schmerzen!*' — 'Aren't you going in, Professor?' asked the Baron. — 'No, no. It's not time yet.' — At last there came from next door an unmistakable cry of '*Oy, vey, vey*!' The doctor threw down his cards and exclaimed: '*Now* it's time.' (SE VIII, 81)

The 'pseudo-joke' rests on the progression, that is — and herein lies the humour — on the regression that takes us from French to German to Yiddish: from the language of high culture to, as Kofman writes, 'the most repressed language', the language that 'resounds (...) from the visceral depths of the unconscious' (PRO, 195).

But it is not so easy to deprive a Jewish story of its Jewish specificity when 'Oy vey' is the utterance that gives the story its oomph. Freud's first move, as always in the *Joke* Book, is universalization. Freud turns the Jewish joke into a universal truth: the joke, he tells us, shows 'how pain causes primitive nature (*ursprüngliche Natur*) to break through all the layers of education, and how an important decision can be properly made to depend on an apparently trivial phenomenon [namely, the shift in idiom]' (SE VIII, 81/GW VI, 87). When the case of this Yiddish-speaking mother returns for the second time, however, a more hostile and more targeted, indeed a more gendered universalization is called for: 'by making the "Oy vey" not a joke but a comic story', Kofman remarks, 'Freud replaces the universal meaning (...) with a more particular meaning: one that no longer brings out the primitive nature (...) of all men (...) but reveals (...) the primitive nature of women' (PRO, 196).

Freud is certainly guilty of universalization and attempted universalization. Though, in a way, you might say that his ambivalence cuts both ways. Freud does not erase the Jewish idiom; the Yiddish words '*Ai, waih, waih* (Oy, vey, vey)' (GW VI, 87) remain perfectly readable in his text. They stand out in German just as they do in French.[9] Having said this, I will emend my statement: the Yiddish words 'Oy, vey, vey' remain both readable and unreadable in Freud's text, readable as unreadable. I say this because James Strachey precisely fails to read them. Strachey is a fabulous translator, as we all know, but, in this case, he gets the joke horribly wrong. Both horribly wrong and horribly right, you might say, since what he reads in Freud's text are not Freud's words but Freud's ambivalence. Indeed, as you will hear, Strachey's translation literally rids the joke of all that is Jewish in it; it actually succeeds, where Freud did not, in erasing the play of the Yiddish idiom. Thus, in Strachey's version of the three cries, the French cry remains unchanged: 'Ah, mon Dieu, que je souffre!' (SE VIII, 81). The German cry, on the other hand, is already a little less German: 'Mein Gott, mein Gott, what terrible pains!' (SE VIII, 81); Strachey assumes, I assume, that well-educated English speakers understand French but not German. But it is the Yiddish cry, the unmistakable Yiddish cry, that becomes not only mistakable but erasable. To the point of being no language at all, that is to say, no human language: 'At last there came (...) an unmistakable cry of "Aa-ee, aa-ee, aa-ee!"'[10]

I think you will agree that this all-vowel cry comes very close to the famous animal sounds in 'Old Macdonald Had a Farm' — E-I-E-I-O' (with a 'moo-moo here and a moo-moo there'). Instead of the Yiddish 'Oy, vey, vey!' that lays bare the 'origins (*ursprüngliche Natur*)' — that is, the Eastern European roots — of the Baroness, Strachey's translation lays bare the animal nature of the woman's childbearing. All pretence falls away *in extremis*, as we learn from the joke, and this seems true for Strachey as well. Indeed, what his 'Aa-ee, aa-ee, aa-ee' conjures up is something mammalian, something like — and the reader will excuse my (veterinary) English — a 'whelping bitch'. But just to be clear: it is not the woman, here, it is the translator who is left with ... let us just call them 'Str(a)tchey-marks'.

Which brings us back to the question of the mother and the Jewish joke. For what we learn from Strachey's (mis)translation is this: that the Jewish joke, engendered by a Jewish mother's 'Oy vey', comes into being through a process that is both idiomatic and unreadable. That is, the Jewish joke is exemplary not because it can be, but because it cannot be, universalized. In the end, the idiom resists translation into concepts; it can and cannot be grasped, pinned down, or formalized by a conceptual analysis — no matter how funny.

Last Word

Nor does mastery of the Yiddish idiom determine what is Jewish. Let me end with one final Jewish joke; I want to take seriously Sarah Kofman's last words in *Pourquoi rit-on?* — 'laissons donc au rire le dernier mot (let us leave the last word to the joke)' (PRO, 198). Believe it or not it is a Jewish joke that makes fun of the loss of the 'Jewish' idiom. A Jew goes to an orthodox rabbi and asks him to pronounce his *brocha* (his blessing or benediction) upon the Jaguar he has just bought. But the orthodox rabbi refuses to give his blessing to a wild animal. The Jew then goes to a conservative rabbi to get the *brocha* for his Jaguar, but the conservative rabbi refuses to bless an automobile. Finally, the Jew goes to a reform rabbi to get his *brocha*. The reform rabbi says: 'I know what a Jaguar is, but what's a *brocha*?'[11]

NOTES

1 See Jacques Derrida's homage to Kofman in Sarah Kofman, *Selected Writings*, translated by Pascale-Anne Brault and Michael Naas, edited by Thomas Albrecht, with Georgia Albert and Elizabeth Rottenberg (Stanford, CA: Stanford University Press, 2007), 7; Sarah Kofman, *Rue Ordener, rue Labat* (Paris: Galilée, 1994), 95, and *Rue Ordener, Rue Labat*, translated by Ann Smock (Lincoln, NE: University of Nebraska Press, 1996), 81, hereafter RO;

page numbers are to the French-language edition followed by the English-language edition.

2 For his part, Winnicott speaks of 'relief' from 'reality-acceptance'. See D. W. Winnicott, *Playing and Reality* (New York: Routledge, 1989), 13.

3 In the case of *Pourquoi rit-on?* it is interesting to note that Kofman's back and forth with Freud describes not only what she does in the book with Freud's texts but also the writing of the book itself, namely, the uncanny way in which Kofman repeats, with Freud, in his wake, the back and forth that distinguishes the writing of *Jokes and Their Relation to the Unconscious* from any of Freud's other books. Indeed, just as Freud goes back and forth between two books (between *Jokes and Their Relation to the Unconscious* and the *Three Essays on the Theory of Sexuality*, which were written simultaneously), so too does Sarah Kofman. In the case of Kofman, the two books are *Pourquoi rit-on?* and *Paroles suffoquées*. In a radio interview, she talks about the simultaneous writing of these two books: 'I wrote [*Paroles suffoquées*] in an extremely depressive state and I experienced a kind of quasi-manic elation in writing on jokes (. . .) [H]aving written the two books simultaneously, I felt at peace with myself for the first time in my life, psychologically, I mean. I was in an extreme state of euphoria after having written the two books at the same time.' In other words, Kofman's book on jokes singularly repeats the originary bi-textuality of Freud's *Joke* Book. For a transcript of Kofman's radio interview, see Ginette Michaud and Isabelle Ullern, *Sarah Kofman et Jacques Derrida: croisements, écarts, différences* (Paris: Hermann, 2018), 278n. 305, my translation, hereafter SKJD.

4 Kofman, *Pourquoi rit-on? Freud et le mot d'esprit* (Paris: Galilée, 1986), 13, my translation, hereafter PRO.

5 Sigmund Freud, 'Preface to Reik's *Ritual: Psychoanalytic Studies*' in *The Standard Edition of the Complete Psychological Works of Sigmund Freud*, translated by James Strachey, 24 volumes (London: Hogarth Press, 1953–74), XVII, 261; Sigmund Freud, 'Vorrede zu *Probleme der Religionspsychologie* von Dr. Theodor Reik' in *Gesammelte Werke*, 18 volumes (Frankfurt am Main: Fischer, 1947), XII, 327, hereafter SE and GW, respectively.

6 Sigmund Freud, *The Complete Letters of Sigmund Freud to Wilhelm Fliess 1887–1904*, edited and translated by Jeffrey Moussaieff Masson (Cambridge, MA: Harvard University Press, 1985), 254, modified, hereafter CL. For more on Freud's Jewish jokes, see Elliott Oring, *The Jokes of Sigmund Freud: A Study in Humor and Jewish Identity* (University Park, PA: University of Pennsylvania Press, 1984), 3–4, hereafter JSF.

7 Both of Freud's parents were Galician Jews. His mother came from the town of Brody and his father from Tysmenytsia.

8 PRO, 32, 36, 66, 68, 96, 99, 110, 132, 165, 183.

9 In all the French translations of *Der Witz und seine Beziehung zum Unbewußten*, the Yiddish remains perfectly readable: 'Ai, ai waih' (Paris: Gallimard, 1930),

'Aï, waïh, waïh!' (Paris: Gallimard, 1988), 'Ai, waih, waih' (Paris: Presses universitaires de France, 2014). See Sigmund Freud, *Le Mot d'esprit et ses rapports avec l'inconscient*, translated by M. Bonaparte and M. Nathan (Paris: Gallimard, 1930), 73, *Le Mot d'esprit et sa relation à l'inconscient*, translated by Denis Messier (Paris: Gallimard, 1988), 162, and *Le Trait d'esprit et sa relation à l'inconscient*, translated by J. Altounian, P. Haller, D. Hartmann, C. Jouanlanne, F. Kahn, R. Lainé, A. Rauzy and F. Robert, in *Œuvres complètes de Freud: Psychanalyse*, edited by A. Bourguignon, P. Cotet and J. Laplanche, 21 volumes (Paris: Presses universitaires de France, 2014), VII, 96.

10 In its proliferation and modulation of vowels, A. A. Brill's translation of this passage goes even further. By confusing the woman's cries with the cries of an animal (or a prelinguistic child), Brill's translation brings out the primal scream of the woman in labour but also, unwittingly, the pains of a man labouring to get the joke: '*At last, there rang from the adjacent room the unmistakable cry, "A-a-a-ai-e-e-e-e-e-e-E-E-E!*"' Sigmund Freud, 'Wit and Its Relation to the Unconscious' in *The Basic Writings of Sigmund Freud*, edited and translated by A. A. Brill (New York: Modern Library, 1995), 649. In her far superior translation, Joyce Crick reproduces the Yiddish in its German transliteration and offers — in brackets — not one but two possibilities of anglicization: ' — Finally, from the next room they hear an unmistakable cry of "*Ai, waih, waih* [equivs: 'O weh', 'Oy vay']".' Sigmund Freud, *The Joke and Its Relation to the Unconscious*, translated by Joyce Crick (New York: Penguin Books, 2003), 83n. 7, 68.

11 Theodor Reik, *Jewish Wit* (New York: Gamut Press, 1962), 87.

And Yet It Quakes! (Nietzsche and Voltaire)

SARAH KOFMAN

For Annie Nogaret

Earthquakes

Each of them was overwhelmed by an earthquake. Voltaire, by that of Lisbon (1 November 1755), Nietzsche, by that of Ischia (28 July 1883). For the former, the *Funeral Oration to Lisbon*, the *Poem on the Disaster of Lisbon* and the correspondence of November 1755 bear witness to this. In a letter to Jean-Robert Tronchin, 24 November 1755, among others, Voltaire writes: 'Behold, Sir, a very cruel physics. We might struggle to comprehend exactly how the laws which govern movement allow for such frightful disasters in the best of all possible worlds. One hundred thousand ants, our neighbours, all crushed in a single blow to our anthill, and half of them doubtlessly perishing in unspeakable anguish, buried amidst rubble from which none could pull them; families ruined at the feet of Europe, the fortunes of hundreds of merchants from your homeland lost in the ruins of Lisbon. What a bitter game of chance human life is!'

In a letter to Peter Gast, 16 August 1883, Nietzsche, for his part, writes: 'The fate of Ischia overwhelms me more and more.'[1] Yet neither Voltaire nor Nietzsche stops at these 'humanitarian' considerations. In the rest of the letter cited above, Voltaire protects himself against the melancholy that might have overcome him by directing a sarcastic irony against those whom, later, he will call the 'Infâmes', fanatics of all kinds. He takes pleasure in imagining that the inquisitor-priests, just like other men, have been crushed, even if, through bad luck, the Palace of the Inquisition had remained standing:

Paragraph 44.1 (2021): 117–137
DOI: 10.3366/para.2021.0358

www.euppublishing.com/para

'This ought to teach men not to persecute men, because, while a few damned scoundrels burn a few fanatics, the earth engulfs both groups.' In a letter to François-Louis Allamand, 16 December 1755, whilst he laments the Portuguese, he consoles himself by judging that, after all, 'moral evil' provokes greater disasters than natural catastrophes do: 'Men do still more harm to themselves upon this little molehill than nature does to them. Our wars slaughter more men than are swallowed up in earthquakes. If we had nothing to fear in this world but the adventure in Lisbon, we would still find ourselves fairly well off.'[2]

The earthquake in Lisbon is, for Voltaire, above all an occasion through which to wage war against the optimism of Leibniz, as he will later do in *Candide* where, at the end of Chapter V and at the beginning of Chapter VI, the earthquake, which had destroyed three-quarters of Lisbon, is evoked so as to denounce the 'wise men' of the country by ridiculing them. In order to prevent total ruin these last had come up with only one remedy: the ceremonial spectacle of a few people being slowly burnt ('doing evil for the pleasure of doing it', Nietzsche will say in the *Second Essay on the Genealogy of Morality*, taking up an expression from Mérimée[3]). These were superb *autos-da-fé*, at which both God and the men who 'for the sake of charity cast their neighbours into the flames' could rejoice.[4] And yet this medicine was totally ineffective: the earth continued to quake!: 'The man from Biscay and the two men who had not wanted to eat bacon were burned; and Pangloss was hanged, despite the fact that this was contrary to custom. The same day the earth quaked once more with a most fearful din.'[5]

As for Nietzsche, he is 'rattled' by the fate of Ischia, 'as any human being might be', but the earthquake that afflicts the island has him turn his gaze in the direction of the superman (*surhumain*). There is, he writes, 'something in the event that hits very near home where I am concerned, and in a peculiarly terrible way'. He is struck by the 'coincidence' of the date of the tremor in Ischia with the completion of his *Zarathustra*, which itself coincided with the death of Wagner: 'I am very taken with this island: when you have read *Zarathustra II* through to the end, it will be clear to you where I have located my Blessed Isles. *"Cupid Dancing with the Young Girls"* can only be understood immediately in Ischia (. . .). Just as my poem was completed, the island went to pieces. You know that at the very hour I finished my first *Zarathustra*, Wagner died'[6] (SLL, 161).

If the earth quaked that very day, at Ischia, it was in face of the immensity of *Zarathustra*, as, long ago, the Jews quaked before the immensity of God. Or rather, this tremor ought to be read as sign heralding the great event of which *Zarathustra* is also a prelude. It announces symbolically the terrible event of the transvaluation of values, the act of humanity's supreme turning back upon itself, comparable to an earthquake (*Krampf*) which shakes all things from the ground up; a shaking that upends everything, reversing all meaning, the consequence of a struggle (*Kampf*) led by Nietzsche against millennia of lies (the very same that, under the name 'Infâmes', Voltaire had himself, in his own way, striven to 'crush').[7]

In the closing pages of 'Why I Write Such Good Books' in *Ecce Homo*, Nietzsche writes that the transvaluation of values 'will plunge the earth into terrible convulsions', because it will be comparable to a shattering lightning bolt (EH, 143). The image of explosives, borrowed from Emerson, seems to dominate here ('I am not a human being, I am dynamite', he says, so as to describe the upending effect of a shock propelling humanity into a new era, that of the Anti-Christ). But this image is accompanied by that of an earthquake which should henceforth also be associated with the name Nietzsche, as with the memory of a prodigious, even monstrous event, a great overwhelming, a true revolution linked to a 'great politics' that no small politician would ever have dared to dream of. The tremor 'prophesied' by Nietzsche, much more powerful than that of Lisbon or Ischia (which would be signs heralding it, its emblems), should make possible the advent of another type of mankind at the antipodes of that fashioned by the ascetic ideal, the result of twenty centuries of Christianity. 'Deciphered' in this way, the earthquake of Ischia vindicates Voltaire: the priests of the Inquisition had not discovered an infallible secret for preventing the earth from quaking, and God, to whom they had offered spectacular *autos-da-fé*, was himself utterly dead, under the effect of a tremor unlike any other.

An Anniversary Gift (Un cadeau d'anniversaire)

In the 'Preface' to *Human, All Too Human*, written after the fact in 1886, Nietzsche was already comparing the paramount event of the advent of Free Spirit, that of a great emancipation from moral and idealist enslavements, to the shock of an earthquake: 'young souls are in a single blow shaken, detached, torn out. They themselves do not understand what is happening.'[8] The earthquake which took place in the period of *Human, All Too Human*, signifies the 'first explosion of strength and autonomy' (HA, 7), the will to liberation that ordered Nietzsche to then cut the umbilical cord linking him to everything with which he had been symbiotically united, particularly Wagner. If *Zarathustra* and the earthquake that accompanied it coincided with Wagner's empirical and symbolic death, a condition of possibility for Nietzsche giving birth to a son who was truly his own, then *Human, All Too Human* is the book of a cathartic crisis, and the first step in the rupture with Wagner, with everything this name was beginning to signify for Nietzsche, with everything that was preventing his advent to himself.[9]

It is hardly surprising therefore that he aims this book at those he calls 'free spirits', an expression that he understands completely differently to David Strauss's 'free thinkers' (EH, 114). In *Beyond Good and Evil*, particularly in paragraph 44 of the chapter on the 'Free Spirit', Nietzsche attempts to dispel all misunderstanding over this term which is abused, he says, in all the countries of Europe and in America.[10] These spirits, falsely said to be free, belong to a species of levellers. They are loquacious slaves, scribblers in the service of democratic taste and its modern ideas. They wrongly see, in the extant structures of society, the almost exclusive cause of every human misery and wrongdoing, 'which is nothing other than to merrily put truth on its head and its feet in the air!' Their aim is to bring about the happiness of the flock, equality of rights, and pity for all those who suffer. The philosophers of the future, of which Nietzsche gives himself as the first precursor, are completely different to these *liberi pensatori*, these *Freidenker*, or whatever other name these excellent defenders of 'modern ideas' might like to give themselves. They will not merely be free, but *very* free spirits, something more, higher, greater, radically different.

The true 'free spirit' who disdains to make himself available, as his coarser brother does, to the veneration of the masses, and whose way of living and thinking is that of a refined, aristocratic heroism (HA, 134), is first of all he who, after having been captured by foreign forces, has been capable of liberating himself and taking possession of himself (EH, 115).

Now, the 'free spirit' — understood in this way — to which Nietzsche dedicates *Human, All Too Human* is precisely Voltaire, whom he judges one of the greatest liberators of spirit.

Of course, after the fact, the 'Preface' of 1886 transforms the 'free spirits to whom this book of courage and discouragement (. . .) is dedicated' into pure fictions, simple spectres and phantoms whom Nietzsche found necessary 'in order to keep [his] good temper while surrounded by bad tempers' (HA, 6). It transforms them into brave accomplices with whom he can laugh and chatter as compensation for an extreme isolation, to which he needed to turn a blind eye: 'Thus when I needed to I once also invented for myself the "free spirits" to whom this book is dedicated (. . .): "free spirits" of this kind do not exist, have never existed.' The future alone, he hopes, might see their advent 'in flesh and bone'.

According to the reading of 1886, Voltaire as 'free spirit' would have, therefore, a purely spectral reality. Furthermore, had Nietzsche not received on 30 May 1878 a bust of Voltaire, an anonymous delivery from Paris, accompanied with a card bearing simply these words: 'The soul of Voltaire pays respects to Friedrich Nietzsche' (see letter to Peter Gast, 31 May 1878)?[11] A strange present which confirms, as though in advance, that the 'Voltaire' to whom *Human, All Too Human* was dedicated was indeed purely phantasmatic. But which perhaps came to haunt him in order to reclaim its due, protesting, before the fact, against a future gesture of reappropriation: that of the 'Preface' of 1886, but also the gesture which *Ecce Homo* will turn into a general one. Nietzsche's various identificatory models are there reduced to simple rungs, to preliminary stages, to bridges leading him to 'himself'.[12] These models are reduced to simple occasional accessories, masks, metaphors for 'himself'; they anticipate this 'self' only insofar as he would have already, without being aware of this, 'transported' it into them, and already made, under their name, his 'own' voice understood.

Putting 'Voltaire' at the beginning of one of his writings would not therefore be to pay homage to this figure, so much as to accomplish a step towards himself. In *Ecce Homo* Nietzsche states that 'The name "Voltaire" on one of my writings (*Schrift*) that was true progress (*Fortschritt*) — towards myself', playing upon the phonic proximity of *Schrift* and *Schritt* in order to bring together (give or take a letter) 'himself' and the dedicatee to whom he pays homage only because he sees himself in him with the greatest exactitude (EH, 116). This is give or take small details: a difference which allows him to loan out his name, with Nietzsche, who associates his name and Voltaire's for all time, ultimately giving a wonderful gift.

More precisely, an anniversary gift.

The occasion of the dedication is, in fact, the hundredth anniversary of the death of Voltaire, as the epigraph to *Human, All Too Human* recalls:

'In memory of Voltaire for the hundredth anniversary of his death, 30 May 1778.

This monological book, which came into being during a winter residence in Sorrento (1876 to 1877), would not have been given to the public at this time if the proximity of the 30th of May 1878 had not aroused all too intensely the wish to offer a timely personal homage to the greatest liberator of the human spirit.'[13]

We know the almost obsessional care which Nietzsche took to celebrate all birthdays, those of his family and his friends — his fear that someone might forget to wish him well on his own, and the importance he placed on the gifts he asked for or received on this occasion.[14] He himself would often give his own books as presents to his friends and then, at his moment of extreme solitude, to humanity in its entirety, so that it might again begin a new era. He always saw the wishes presented as a guarantee of survival for the year to come, a type of guarantee against death. Giving to Voltaire, on the hundredth anniversary of his death, *Human, All Too Human* would not therefore signify a simple passing homage, provoked by the occasion, but a will to immortalize the greatest liberator of spirit, the will for his eternal return.

After the fact, of course, Nietzsche will reduce 'Voltaire' to a pure step towards the becoming 'Nietzsche' of Nietzsche. However, he constantly has him 'come back' in his work: he leaves him not the last word, but the second to last, since it is precisely prior to the lapidary final slogan: 'Dionysus against the Crucified', that he reappropriates, once more, the Voltairean watchword: 'Écrasez l'infâme!' (EH, 151). To do so is to eternally put into the dock of infamies a morality unable to distinguish between what is and is not *infâme*, and in order to wither with a crushing motto a morality which itself has made the most beautiful plants of humanity wither.

The final reprise of Voltaire's polemical slogan with which, from the 1760s through to the end of his life, he stamped his correspondence, echoing that of the Roman Cato ('Carthage must be destroyed'), is not without a certain displacement in relation to the meaning that Voltaire had given to it.[15] (The phrase shows, above all, his violent indignation against religious superstitions and their absurdities, against fanaticism and intolerance: he had exhorted a 'fraternal' community, united against the *Infâmes*, to crush them at any price, but he never attacked, under this name, morality properly speaking, which on the contrary he was concerned with preserving.)

There was also a displacement in relation to the meaning that Nietzsche conferred upon this phrase at the moment of *Human, All Too Human* where, in Voltaire's footsteps, he called for support of the 'spirit of the Enlightenment' and progressive evolution, which according to him had long been driven back by the optimistic spirit of the Revolution and its idealistic lies, which it owed to Rousseau: 'It is up to us to see — each on his account — whether it is possible to call it back' (§463 (HA, 169)). In this same text in which he accuses Rousseau, he pays homage to Voltaire, who is described as a 'measured nature, given to regularising, purifying, reconstructing'.

Of the Lordly Tone of a 'joyful monster'

In spite of these different interpretations given to the 'same' slogan (and we know that, for Nietzsche, a statement has no meaning in 'itself', but as many meanings as there are strangleholds upon it by this or that force), the fact that Nietzsche took it up even in his very last texts underlines a profound affinity between the relentless struggle of the 'immoralist' and Voltaire's struggle against all infamies, even if the latter did not push his critical spirit far enough or radically enough for him to have perceived that the morality in whose name he was fighting also had a part in the greatest of infamies.

When rereading his work after the fact, Nietzsche of course strives to make Voltaire into a simple mask behind which he sheltered so as to make his own voice understood. But it is not by chance that he was forced, at the moment of his initial affirmation of autonomy, to take up the mask of another; nor was it by chance that this mask was that of Voltaire.

At the moment of *Human, All Too Human*, it is indeed in 'Voltaire' that Nietzsche sees 'himself' the most, almost as his double. He recognizes essentially a certain accent, a certain timbre of his voice, a certain tone which he did not yet know to be 'his' and which puts him in kinship with Voltaire: the tone of a cold, hard and mocking intelligence, the very tone of a 'critical' spirit which rends up like a ploughshare, rends itself up, sets to work on the question whilst calling itself into question; the tone of a scalpel-wielder, icy and pitiless (EH, 116). Under cover of the name of Voltaire, this pitiless spirit wages war against — and pursues through to its last entrenchments — the ideal, whatever mask it wears and wherever it might seek to hide itself (in morality, in religion, but also in art, science, philosophy, in certain supposed enemies of idealism). Nietzsche ascribes this tone of critical intellectuality to an aristocratic taste: it is a 'lordly tone', which distinguishes Voltaire from all subsequent writers and puts him in kinship only with his own nobility of spirit.[16]

Attaching the critical spirit to aristocratism can seem surprising if we recall this or that text by Nietzsche which links Voltaire to a plebeian Socrates and his dialectics, and where Socrates is described as a *buffo* with the instincts of Voltaire tagged on.[17] But, according to Nietzsche, the intellectuality of Voltaire (and his own) is superior and noble because it manifests itself through a distancing from any passionate foundation, over which it wins a victory. Furthermore, it provides, after a cathartic, 'negative' moment, affirmative happiness and wellbeing. The final attitude of aristocratic intellectuality is that of a contradiction that contradicts no more, a neutrality which has learnt to say yes.

In the end, this noble distancing manifests itself through the invention — common to Voltaire and Nietzsche — of an antidote against the potentially destructive elements within the critical spirit, and within 'rationalism' pushed to the extreme: laughter, which 'saves' each of them from melancholic bitterness and from pessimism. Nietzsche notes that, around 1770, a decline in joyfulness was already observable (women, for their part, had thought wrongly that immorality was to blame . . .) and, following Galiani, he takes pleasure in citing Voltaire's lines:

'A joyful monster is worth more / Than any sentimental bore' (WP, 62).

In the same unpublished fragment, he underlines his profound complicity with Voltaire: the invention of an antidote was even more necessary for him than for his 'double', his rationalism and the pessimism it led to being so much more radical, so much more excessive because they could only be tolerated through this inspired remedy. 'Now, if I imagine that I have a few centuries' advance upon the rationalism of Voltaire and even Galiani — who was much more profound — how much more bitter than them ought I be?[18] This, furthermore, is true: I have, in time, and not without some regret, taken my precautions against German and Christian meanness, against illogicality, against Schopenhauerian or even Leopardian pessimism, and I have gone in search of the original forms of pessimism (in Asia). But so as to bear this excess of pessimism (as transpires here and in my

The Birth of Tragedy), so as to live alone, "without god and without morality", I had to invent for myself an antidote. *Perhaps I know better than anybody why man is the only being that knows how to laugh* (emphasis mine [S. K.]): he alone suffers profoundly enough to have been forced to invent laughter. The most ill-fortunate, the most melancholic of all animals is, as is just, the most joyful' (WP, 62).

The essential battle-weapon of Voltaire enabling him to rise up against every serious spirit and against every bore was, indeed, nothing other than laughter. It was through joyfulness and laughter that he thought himself assured of triumph and victory in the war against the *Infâme*. The correspondence bears witness to this. For example, in a letter to Thiriot, 19 May 1760, he writes: 'I advise all philosophers to make a mockery of their enemies, this world is a war, those who laugh at the expense of others are victorious.' And the same day, to L. F. d'Épinay, he writes: 'One must laugh at everything, that is the only good approach.' Two days later, to D'Alembert, he gives the same advice, adding that a true philosopher is surely also someone who laughs and declaring that he, for his part, wishes to die laughing. He recommends to D'Alembert, who was 'born joyful', to make a mockery of all the wretches who attack philosophy, and to employ himself with joyfully destroying the *Infâme*: 'Laugh, laugh and you crush them.' On 30 June 1760, again to D'Alembert, he declares that for six months he has had an urge to laugh which has not left him.

To Thiriot, 29 August 1760, he confides that Jean-Jacques has gone mad by dint of being serious and that he is very far from laughing.

To the Comtesse d'Argental, 13 October 1760, he affirms that he was born light-hearted and that he regrets having sometimes devoted himself to seriousness.

To Damilaville, 24 January 1763, with regard to his *Treatise on Tolerance*, he underlines that there are some places which will make him quiver with fright and others that will make him quiver with laughter, because: 'Thank God, intolerance is as absurd as it is horrible.'

To D'Alembert, 31 December 1763, he states that he is so disgusted with what people call serious things that he has started writing some *Tales of Mother Goose*.

The Voltaire–Rousseau Agon

Whilst, through all of these aspects, Nietzsche feels himself so connected to Voltaire that he makes him one of his multiple 'incarnations', the agonal confrontation between Rousseau and Voltaire serves as a decisive countercheck. According to Nietzsche, in fact, the way one reacts to this celebrated contest is fundamental in knowing *who* one is, and the difference that follows from whether the one or the other is endorsed is considerable. The Voltaire–Rousseau confrontation can serve as a criterion, as a typological distinction, because a choice in favour of one or other signals a kinship with either the 'aristocracy' or the 'plebeians'.

As such, the enemies of Voltaire (for example, Victor Hugo and the Romantics, even the subtler sort, such as the Goncourt brothers) are all favourably disposed to the 'masked plebeian' that Rousseau is, and their Romanticism is said to consist, perhaps completely, in plebeian rancour. Voltaire, for his part, belongs only to intellectual roguery: 'He is a witty, splendid rogue and is only possible or sufferable in the frame of an aristocratic civilisation which can allow itself the luxury of "intellectual roguery".'[19]

Just as Voltaire and Rousseau constantly fought with one another from 1760 onwards, Nietzsche constantly confronts, typologically, the *Lord* of Ferney and the *Citizen* of Geneva, always in support of the former.

He notes initially that it was the intense agonal rivalry of the aristocrat and the plebeian that was the greatest stimulant to Voltaire's becoming 'Voltaire': his envy, his hatred of Rousseau's success are claimed to be what drove Voltaire to become the man of his century, the representative of tolerance and unbelief where before he had only been a fine wit (WP, 69). This *agon* with the plebeian pushed the aristocrat, a representative of the victorious and dominant castes, onwards towards the heights, while Rousseau remained 'untouched' by this struggle, remained plebeian even as a man of letters, scorning in an impudent and unheard-of way everything he was not himself.[20]

This typological reading is accompanied, as ever, by a 'medical' diagnostic: 'Rousseau was *sickly* (and this sickliness is his most imitated feature; we find it again with Lord Byron; he too artificially raised himself up to sublime attitudes). (...) In Rousseau, there was undoubtedly mental disorder (...). The rancour of the sick: these periods of insanity are also those of his misanthropy and distrust' (WP, 70).

With Voltaire, on the contrary, there is claimed to have been an unusual health and ease. Understand: 'great health', since, as his correspondence reveals, he was in fact more and more encumbered, like Nietzsche, with physical ailments. But this sickliness did not prevent him from continuing to laugh at everything, quite the opposite, and this through to his death bed since he is said to have ended his life on a *bon mot* ridiculing God. Nietzsche recalls this at a moment when he himself is campaigning against the Christian ideal — the doctrine which makes beatitude and salvation the aim of life — and rising up against the supremacy of the simple-witted, the pure in heart, sufferers, and the indigent, reducing the existence of God to that of a simple, fading word: 'what is God or faith in God to us now! "God" today is merely a faded word, not even a concept. But as Voltaire said on his deathbed: "Don't speak to me about him!" When and where have we seen a man worthy of the name bear the least resemblance to the Christian ideal? At least if we see things as the psychologists do, those triers of hearts and kidneys! Have a skim through Plutarch's *Lives*' (WP, 138).

When Nietzsche affirms therefore in *The Anti-Christ* that a God so pale and so anaemic would need to be annulled even if he did exist, he is not actually opposed to Voltaire, who proclaims that if God did not exist he would need to be invented.[21] Because, as he recalls elsewhere, Voltaire judges this invention necessary only for the riff-raff who need to believe in a rewarding and avenging god (WP, 70): 'It is indubitable that it is infinitely more useful in a lawful city to have a religion (even a bad one) than to have none at all.'[22]

As an aristocrat, gifted like Nietzsche with an unparalleled instinct for genealogy, Voltaire makes keen distinctions, if not between the 'nobles' and the plebeians, then at least between 'illuminated' people, 'philosophers', 'honourable people', on the one hand and on the other, the uncultured riff-raff who, so as to respect social morality, must believe in God and Hell.[23] In the article 'Hell' in the *Philosophical Dictionary*, Voltaire puts in the mouth of a priest this profession of (non-)faith: 'I don't believe in an eternal hell any more than you; but it is a good thing for your servant, your tailor and even your lawyer to believe in it' (PD, 186).[24]

As Nietzsche underlines, Voltaire is indeed fighting, essentially, for the preservation of society, for the cause of 'honourable people' and 'fine company', for the very cause of progress and civilization. The invention of society, according to him, is the finest invention of all, and there would be no higher goal than maintaining and perfecting it: 'This is precisely what is laudable about the observation of social practices, just as virtue consists in obedience to certain necessary prejudices which favour the conservation of society' (WP, 70).

Rousseau states that mankind perfects itself in the degree to which it approaches nature; according to Voltaire, on the contrary, mankind perfects itself in the degree to which it distances itself from nature. The very same periods which are, for the one, those of humanity's progress are, for the other, those in which injustice and inequality get worse.

Contra Rousseau, Voltaire states that the primitive state of nature is dreadful, that man is a wild beast, that our civilization is an unheard-of triumph over this nature as wild beast: 'He experienced the ameliorations, the refinements, the intellectual joys of the civilised state; he scorned the limited spirit, even when this appears under the cloak of virtue; and the lack of delicacy, even in ascetics and monks. Rousseau seemed to be preoccupied with the moral wretchedness of man; it is with the words "unjust" and "cruel" that the instincts of the oppressed, who would ordinarily find themselves under the constraints of the *vetitum* and of the fear of disgrace, are best stimulated' (WP, 69).[25]

Rousseau thinks that mankind alone has corrupted mankind and pleads in favour of a providentialism which is set in opposition to the pessimism of Voltaire and his belief in social progress alone.

Beyond Voltaire and Rousseau

In the contest that sets Voltaire in opposition to Rousseau, Nietzsche always takes the side of the former, a stance that classes him typologically; he resists, however, any pure or simple assimilation to this figure who served him as model and as frontman in the period of *Human, All Too Human*. He situates himself, through his virile scepticism, beyond both Rousseau's optimism and Voltaire's pessimism, rejecting them both as one. Whilst he does not advocate a 'turning back' that is characteristic — according to Voltaire — of Rousseau's position, neither does he accept a Voltairean conception of 'progress': that modern, all too modern idol which he tramples upon just as much as the idols of the past (AC, 5). What most differentiates Nietzsche from Voltaire is precisely this: the only progress that Nietzsche conceives of is a 'return to nature', understood not as a regression but as a 'march forwards, towards the heights, towards a sublime, free, and even terrible nature (. . .) which plays, and has the right to play, at great tasks'.[26] The only progress conceivable is that of a displacement of mankind by itself which would have it become more profound, more immoral, stronger, more confident in itself, and to this degree more natural (WP, 81).

Voltaire's mistake, like that of Rousseau, is to have believed in a radical opposition between culture and nature, whereas, according to Nietzsche, society is not something that could either perfect nature or corrupt it, but is itself a natural power. Its 'educative' task is the very same as that of 'Nature', and it uses the same means. This is why Nietzsche considers that the essential problem of civilization remains, following Voltaire and Rousseau, an unresolved problem.

Voltaire, so as to attempt to resolve this problem, makes the mistake of approaching things from too human a perspective, thus subordinating his research in a positivistic way to utility and to the good.

And if Nietzsche rejoices when the Lord of Ferney still comprehends *umanità* in the sense of the Renaissance, and likewise *virtù* (as 'superior culture') (WP, 69), he nevertheless judges his 'humanitarianism' to be foolish, and a fundamental obstacle to his search for truth: 'O Voltaire, O humanitarianism, O foolishness! There is something to "truth" and to the search for truth; and when a man takes this up in too human a way— when "il ne cherche le vrai que pour le bien" (in French) — I bet he won't find anything' (BGE, 35).[27] Or he will only find a few 'human, all too human' truths of a size befitting 'mankind', that 'homunculus'.[28] As such, unlike Voltaire, Nietzsche dares not take the 'side of humanity' against all those who, like the 'sublime misanthropist' that Pascal was according to Voltaire, judge men too wretched or too misfortunate.[29] Because, so as to prevent mankind from remaining forever the 'sublime runt' bequeathed by the ascetic ideal (BGE, 57), one must instead learn to make mankind more beautiful, stronger, and as such more malicious, more confident in the powers which until now it transferred onto divinity, emptying itself of them. And to this end, it must put itself to a harsh schooling: that of the philosopher god Dionysus, whom Nietzsche gives himself as the last disciple of (TI, 229), whom he makes his last 'incarnation'. He makes Dionysus his last borrowed name, signifying an acquiescence to life without reserve, breaking with all pessimism as with all optimism, because the *amor fati* of Nietzsche wishes for the eternal return of life even in its terrible and frightening aspects, without making these an argument against its existence, but quite on the contrary a further reason to affirm it.

Writing to Cosima Wagner on 3 January 1889 (under the name of Princess Ariadne, his beloved), Nietzsche reveals the multiple identities which break him apart as a united subject identical to itself in the course of time, and also as a man, since this category has always presupposed a specific difference guaranteeing the human species an identity distinguishing it from others, from animality or from divinity: 'It is a prejudice that I am a man. But I have often lived among men and I have known everything that men can experience from the most lowly to the most high. I have been Buddha among the Indians, Dionysus in Greece, Alexander and Caesar are my incarnations, the same as the poet behind Shakespeare, Lord Bacon. Lastly, I was Voltaire and Napoleon, perhaps Richard Wagner ... But this time, I come as Dionysus victorious who will transform the earth into celebration ... Not that I shall have very much time ... The skies rejoice that I am here ... I have also been hanged from the cross.'[30]

Dionysus victorious will not transform the earth into a celebration without having initially made it quake a great deal: because what this 'type' of God incarnates is the most unheard-of alliance of destruction and affirmation, an overabundance of affirmative and destructive forces capable of having the entire earth explode, propelling it into a new era. In his destructive aspect, Dionysus is a god of nocturnal darkness, as was underlined in a lecture course delivered at Basel, in 1875: 'Dionysus himself is *Zeus nukios*, Nocturnal Zeus. (...) He is a god of the nocturnal skies, of darkness, of stormy weather, of night, of the underworld; therefore Sabus Dionysus is more important, more powerful than the God of the pure, beautiful sky of day.'[31]

The language of Dionysus is no longer that of words, not even 'bons mots', but that of lightning bolts, the roaring of thunder, terrifying explosions and earthquakes. He prevents one from sheltering from excessively unpleasant 'truths' — no longer appropriately sized for mankind and the prejudices necessary to its conservation, but 'immoralist' truths which cast off all security in shaking the very being of mankind from the ground up.

At the end of *Ecce Homo*, Nietzsche affirms once again his kinship with Voltaire by attaching to the famous Voltairean watchword his own battle-slogan: 'Dionysus against the crucified' (EH, 151). But this is also to underline the advance that has been made since *Human, All Too Human*: the name 'Voltaire' was perhaps therefore a simple temporary shelter, a hiding-place in which he could have concealed himself, could have held himself in suspense prior to arriving at 'his own' language and his most appropriate *name*, prior to his advent to 'himself' or to Dionysus. A hiding-place which already allowed him to be joyful and to laugh and to suspect that the earth could become something other than an 'ascetic star': 'A little corner inhabited by some discontented, arrogant and repugnant creatures who are afflicted with a profound and incurable disgust for themselves, for the earth and for all life and who relentlessly inflict suffering for the pleasure of inflicting suffering, probably their only pleasure' (GM, 85). But the laughter and celebration could truly begin only with a 'crushing' of infamies still more radical than that advocated by Voltaire who, in waging his war against religious superstition and fanaticism, did so in the name of a 'morality' which was, however, indissociable from them, and even their strongest ally, and whose value he never questioned, because in his struggle against the Christian religion, he needed at all costs the support of 'honourable people', for fear of becoming the execration of mankind (see letter to D'Alembert, 13 February 1764), something that Nietzsche, who makes a mockery of 'well-meaning people' (see EH, 'Why I Am a Destiny'), felt weighing upon him as a threat, although without dreading it.

In attacking what Voltaire wanted to keep beyond all suspicion, in putting morality itself into the dock of infamies, Nietzsche invents an attack against Christianity (all of whose strength, in fact, lies in that morality) that is without parallel and infinitely more radical than that of Voltaire. As he writes to Peter Gast, 26 August 1883: 'I am one of the most terrible adversaries of Christianity, and have invented a mode of attack of which even Voltaire himself had no idea' (SLL, 164).

Truly, an attack to make the monster it was concerned with crushing quake.

(Translated by JACOB BATES-FIRTH and JOHN McKEANE)

NOTES

1 Friedrich Nietzsche, *Selected Letters*, edited by Oscar Levy, translated by Anthony M. Ludovici (New York and Toronto: Doubleday, Page, 1921), 161, hereafter SLL.

2 See also the letters to Jacob Vernes, 29 January 1756, and to François de Chennevières, 8 February 1756.

3 Friedrich Nietzsche, *On the Genealogy of Morality*, edited by Keith Ansell-Pearson, translated by Carol Diethe (Cambridge: Cambridge University Press, 1997), 41, hereafter GM.

4 Voltaire, 'Poème sur la loi naturelle' in *Œuvres complètes de Voltaire: volume 32B*, edited by David Beeson, Theodore Besterman, Nicholas Cronk, Olivier Ferret, Claude Lauriol, H. T. Mason, Roland Mortier, Ralph Nablow and Thomas Wynn (Oxford: Voltaire Foundation, 2007), 73.

5 Voltaire, *Candide and Other Stories*, translated by Roger Pearson (Oxford: Oxford University Press, 2006), 15.

6 Nietzsche in reality plays fast and loose with the dates, since on 28 July 1883 Peter Gast had already received the proofs to correct in Venice. For Nietzsche's insistence on coincidences, see my *Explosion I* (Paris: Galilée, 1992) and *Explosion II* (Paris: Galilée, 1993).

7 Friedrich Nietzsche, 'Ecce Homo' in *The Anti-Christ, Ecce Homo, Twilight of the Idols, and Other Writings*, edited by Aaron Ridley and Judith Norman, translated by Judith Norman (Cambridge: Cambridge University Press, 2005), 144, hereafter EH.

8 Friedrich Nietzsche, *Human, All Too Human*, translated by R. J. Hollingdale (Cambridge: Cambridge University Press, 1996), 7, hereafter HA.

9 See my *Explosion I* and *II* for the full detail of the relationship between Nietzsche and Wagner.

10 Friedrich Nietzsche, *Beyond Good and Evil*, edited by Rolf-Peter Horstmann and Judith Norman, translated by Judith Norman (Cambridge: Cambridge University Press, 2002), 40–1, hereafter BGE.

11 Friedrich Nietzsche, *Selected Letters*, edited and translated by Christopher Middleton (Indianapolis, IN: Hackett, 1969), 166, hereafter SLM.

12 See *The Voyager and His Shadow*, §210: 'Intemperance in presumptuousness' (HA, 361).

13 Letter to Carl von Gerdorff, 15 April 1876: 'I shall speak to you from Ferney, the residence of Voltaire (to whom I have brought my heartfelt homages).' Friedrich Nietzsche, *Sämtliche Briefe: Band I: Juni 1860–September 1864*, edited by Giorgio Colli and Mazzino Montinari (Berlin: Walter de Gruyter, 1986), 151. (Translators' note: the first line of this dedication is cited in the Hollingdale translation of *Human, All too Human* (HA), xxi. The second paragraph, which Nietzsche removed from the expanded, second edition of the work, is cited in Friedrich Nietzsche, *The Complete Works*, vol. III: *Human, All Too Human I*, translated by Gary Handwerk (Stanford, CA: Stanford University Press, 1997).)

14 See on this subject the chapter 'Des vendanges à la Claude Lorraine' in my *Explosion I*.

15 We should cite practically all the correspondence from 1759 onwards, the year of the suspension of the *Encyclopédie* by the Jesuits, which set Voltaire on a war footing 'in order to protect the living and the dead against the people of the Church' (see a letter to E. N. Damilaville and N. C. Thiriot, 14 May 1761).

In a letter to L. F. d'Épinay, 14 July 1760, Voltaire laments the division of philosophers and in particular Jean-Jacques, whose head has been turned absolutely, which prevents him from being a true ally against the *Infâmes* and the *Infâme*.

In a letter to the same, 10 August 1760, he associates his watchword with that of Cato: 'Destroy the *Infâme*. Such is my opinion, and let us destroy Carthage, in the words of Cato, who was not as old as I am.'

In a letter to E. N. Damilaville and N. C. Thiriot, 31 May 1763, the *Infâme* is presented as a beast to be hunted and which he is concerned with tracking down: 'Make a common, skilful assault on the *Infâme*: that which interests me is the propagation of faith, of truth, the progress of philosophy and the degradation of the *Inf.*'

In a letter to D'Alembert, 17 June 1762: the *Infâme* is compared to a dangerous insect which threatens to sting one in the heel.

In a letter to Damilaville, 9 September 1762, after a publication by a Jesuit priest slandering and denouncing *Voltaire's Mistakes*, a publication consisting in lies and insults, and aiming 'for the greater glory of God', Voltaire states that he has horrified the *Infâme* more than ever.

In a letter to D'Alembert, 15 September 1762, his appeal against the *Infâme* is associated with his defence of Calas: 'Cry out everywhere, I pray to you, for those such as Calas and against fanaticism, because is it the *Infâme* that has caused their misfortune.'

In a letter to D'Alembert, 28 November 1762, it is made clear that, under the name *Infâme*, he is concerned above all with the Jesuits: 'The *Infâme* is much more powerful towards the Danube. You have said to me that it loses its credit towards the Seine. I hope so, but consider that there are three hundred thousand men pledged to sustain this frightful colossus, that is to say more combatants for superstition than France has soldiers. All that gentlemen can do is moan to each other when this superstition becomes persecutory, and to laugh when it is only absurd, to illuminate as many well-born minds (*esprits*) as we can, and to insensibly form, in the minds of men who will go on to have a future, a barrier against this abominable scourge. They should know that without the disputes on transubstantiation or the papal bull, Henri III, Henri IV, and Louis XV would not have been assassinated. (. . .). You know full well that I am speaking only of superstition, because Christian religion I love and respect as you do.'

'(. . .) Protect, my brother, Calas's widow as much as you can. She is an imbecilic Huguenot, but her husband was the victim of the White Penitents. It is important to mankind that the fanatics of Toulouse are defeated. (. . .) Whatever you do, crush the *Infâme.*'

In a letter to Damilaville, 13 December 1762, the exhortation is associated again with the Calas affair and the struggle against intolerance: 'O my brothers, battle the *Inf* . . . through to your last gasp . . .'.

In a letter to the same, 26 December 1762, in this slogan, it is a question of striking a blow against fanaticism, which was very widespread in Languedoc among other places.

In a letter to D'Alembert, 18 January 1763, 'Crush the *Infâme*' again refers to the struggle against the Jesuits, 'who are not yet destroyed'.

In a letter to E. N. Damilaville, 1 December 1763, with regard to a letter from a Quaker, and to the *Treatise on Tolerance*, Voltaire declares that their business is not with Parliament: 'Our great affair is that of crushing the *Inf* . . . ', while avoiding compromising oneself too much.

A letter to D'Alembert, 15 December 1763, finishes with an appeal to a communion of honourable people, involving learning to read the *Holy Scriptures* well and to *crush the Infâme*.

In a letter to the same, 31 December 1763, crushing fanaticism is compared to crushing the Hydra: 'It is always good, from time to time, to cut off a few of the Hydra's heads, even if they will grow back. The monster, in remembering the knife, grows less bold and less insolent, it sees that you hold a club ready to crush it and it quakes.'

In a letter to D'Alembert, 13 February 1764, he insists upon the philosophers' role in crushing the *Infâme*: 'Philosophers certainly will not destroy the Christian religion, but Christianity will not destroy them either, their number will always grow; young people destined for great things will enlighten themselves with them, religion will become less barbaric and society will become gentler. They prevent the priests from corrupting reason and morality. They render fanatics abominable and the superstitious ridiculous. Such is our situation, that mankind will detest us, if we do not have honourable people on our side; we must have them, therefore, whatever the price may be; work in the vineyard therefore, crush the *Infâme*.' In the N.B. the exhortation is repeated.

16 The *Encyclopédie* (in the article 'Lord' (*Grand seigneur*)) distinguishes this last from great man (*grand homme*): '*Lords* are common in the world and *great men* are very rare; the one is sometimes a burden on the State, the other is always a resource and support to it. Birth, titles, and expenses make a *lord*. A *lord* meets the prince, has his ancestors, his debts, and his pensions; a *great man* serves his homeland in a signal way without seeking recompense, without even having any regard for the glory which might come back to him. The Duc d'Épernon and the Maréchal de Retz were *lords*. The Admiral of Coligny was a *great man*.' The French can be found online at https://artflsrv03.uchicago.edu/philologic4/encyclopedie1117/navigate/14/4948/ (consulted on 4 November 2020).

17 Friedrich Nietzsche, *The Will to Power*, edited by R. Kevin Hill, translated by R. Kevin Hill and Michael A. Scarpitti (London: Penguin, 2007), 257, hereafter WP.

18 See BGE, §26. After describing cynicism as the only form under which the souls of the riff-raff might arrive at probity, Nietzsche adds: '(. . .) a superior man should lend his ear and be pleased each time a shameless buffoon or a scientific satyr raises its voice in front of him. There are even cases

where enchantment is mixed with disgust, particularly when genius through a caprice of nature is tied to one of these billy-goats or these impudent apes, as with the Abbé Galiani, the most profound, the most lucid and perhaps the filthiest man of his century; he was much more profound than Voltaire and consequently a great deal less loquacious' (BGE, 28). Marmontel called him a 'Harlequin with the mind of Machiavelli'. Jean François Marmontel, *Memoirs: Volume II* (London: J. Richardson, 1908), 125.

19 For all this, see letter to Peter Gast, 24 November 1887 (SLM, 278).

20 I have shown that in *Ecce Homo* Nietzsche, forced to speak of himself in the first person, something which he had not done through until then, parodied the indecent, 'plebeian' gesture of the Rousseau of the *Confessions* (see my *Explosion I*). Many other points of comparison could be drawn between Rousseau and Nietzsche who, we know, carried within himself a double system of evaluations which made of him, at once, a 'beginning' and a 'decadent' (EH, 75).

21 Friedrich Nietzsche, 'The Anti-Christ' in *The Anti-Christ, Ecce Homo, Twilight of the Idols, and Other Writings*, 52, hereafter AC.

22 Voltaire, *Philosophical Dictionary*, translated by Theodore Besterman (London: Penguin, 1979), 56, hereafter PD.

23 In the 'Preface' to the *Philosophical Dictionary*, Voltaire writes: 'It is even only by illuminated people that this book can be read. The vulgar are not made for such understandings, philosophy will not be their share. Those who say that there are truths that should be hidden from the people ought not to be alarmed; the people will not read them; they work six days a week and go to the cabaret on the seventh. In a word, works of philosophy are only for philosophers and all honourable men ought to seek to be philosophers without priding themselves on being so.' Voltaire, *Philosophical Dictionary* (New York: Carlton House, 1900), 5. (Translators' note: the preface is not included in the version of this *Dictionary* cited above.)

24 As concerns the necessity of the invention of hell for ordinary people, Voltaire cites in the same text the exceptional case of the Jews, the most terrestrial of men, who did not need to invent a completely spiritual system (that of chastisement after life). Among this people, the chastisements were uniquely temporal. Their attachment to life was such (and this here is a point that Nietzsche also insists upon very notably: see my 'Scorning Jews', translated by Ann Smock, in *Selected Writings*, edited by Thomas Albrecht, with Georgia Albert and Elizabeth Rottenberg (Stanford, CA: Stanford University Press, 2007)) that the threat of an enduring temporal malediction was for them the equivalent of a dread of a hell *post mortem*. 'We [Jews] used the word meaning soul only in order to signify *life* (. . .). The distinction between soul and body, the idea of a life after death, can be the fruit only of a long meditation and a very subtle philosophy (. . .). We thought we had done enough in persuading our people that God punishes evil-doers to the fourth generation,

either through leprosy, sudden death or through the loss of what little wealth they were able to possess' (PD, 185).

Many of Voltaire's statements on Jews could be set in parallel with those of Nietzsche. For example, they each underline the contradiction there is in loathing Jews while considering everything they said and wrote to be divine, a contradiction that Europe has inherited even while forgetting that the God of the Christians was, he too, a Jew.

In the article 'Tolerance' in the *Philosophical Dictionary*, Voltaire writes: 'If it were permissible to reason consistently in matters of religion, it would be clear that we should all make ourselves Jews because our saviour J. C. was born a Jew, lived a Jew, died a Jew, and because he said expressly that he accomplished, fulfilled the Jewish religion. But it is clearer still that we should tolerate each other mutually, since we are all weak, inconsistent, subject to mutability and to error' (PD, 393–4).

The text of §44 of *The Anti-Christ* seems to echo this: there Nietzsche writes that Christians are 'Jews, always Jews, still Jews, triply Jews' (AC, 4). See also an unpublished fragment from the period of *Daybreak*: 'Only the Jews have accomplished a Jesus of Nazareth, only they a Holy God, only they sin against God.' Friedrich Nietzsche, *Nachgelassene Fragmente: 1880–1882*, edited by Giorgio Colli and Mazzino Montinari (Berlin: Walter de Gruyter, 1999), 75, hereafter NF.

Voltaire and Nietzsche each also underline the very particular scorn in which the Romans held the Jews (and the Christians to the extent that they are Jewish). Each of them cites the same verse of Horace: 'Credat judaeus Apella[, non ego]' (let the Jew Apella believe it[, not me]). Nietzsche does so in order to show that it is the Jewish demand of faith that above all appears absurd and unbearable to the Romans, writing: 'They are imagined to be capable of believing absurdities in good faith (...). In Jesus Christ, it was the Jew that demanded faith above all. (...) An unbearable demand for faith... "Credat judaeus Apella"' (NF, 76). Voltaire links this citation from Horace with the Romans' profound scorn for Jewish circumcision. Apella was also known as *Curtus Apella* (the shortened, the truncated, the incomplete); in a more general way, the Jews were derisively called *Curti* (*curti Judaei*). In the article 'Circumcision' in the *Philosophical Dictionary*, Voltaire underlines the inconsistency of the Romans, who did not scorn the Egyptians from whom the enslaved Jews had borrowed this custom. And this came, moreover, since the Egyptians had openly revered the instrument of generation whose image they carried with great ceremony in their processions. Voltaire draws from this a conclusion on the general relativity of morality, which instead of leading to scorn for this or that people, should induce a spirit of generalized tolerance: 'Ancient oriental customs are so prodigiously different from ours that nothing can appear extraordinary to anyone who has some reading. A Parisian is taken aback when he is told that the Hottentots cut off one testicle from their male children. The Hottentots are perhaps surprised that the Parisians keep two' (PD, 149).

It would be interesting to compare the respective readings carried out by Voltaire and by Nietzsche of the figure of Saint Paul. They cut across one another on many points.

25 Translators' note: A *vetitum* was a prohibition in the canon law of the Church.

26 See *Skirmishes of an Untimely Man*, §48. Friedrich Nietzsche, 'The Twilight of the Idols' in *The Anti-Christ, Ecce Homo, Twilight of the Idols, and Other Writings*, 221, hereafter TI.

27 In a letter to Frederick, King of Prussia, October 1737, Voltaire writes: 'I have drawn as much as I can my metaphysics from morality.'

28 'Ecce, ecce, homunculus.' Friedrich Nietzsche, *Nachgelassene Fragmente: 1875–1879*, edited by Giorgio Colli and Mazzino Montinari (Berlin: Walter de Gruyter, 1988), 403.

29 Voltaire, 'On the *Pensées* of Pascal' in *Letters on England*, translated by Leonard Tancock (London: Penguin, 2005), 120.

30 Translators' note: Our translation of the original, which can be found here: http://www.nietzschesource.org/#eKGWB/BVN-1889,1241 (consulted on 16 October 2020).

31 Friedrich Nietzsche, *Vorlesungsaufzeichnungen: WS 1874/75–WS 1878/79*, edited by Fritz Bornmann and Mario Carpitelle (Berlin: Walter de Gruyter, 1995), 390–1.

Notes on Contributors

Jacob Bates-Firth is a graduate researcher at the Psychoanalysis Unit, University College London.

Joseph R. Johnson (PhD NYU, 2017) is an Assistant Professor of French and Francophone Studies at Georgetown University. His research explores intersections between medieval literature and poetry, on the one hand, and questions that cut across the history of philosophy on the other — especially the question of how language's materiality complicates or disrupts efforts of conscious expression. He has published on the resonance of medieval language with the ethical framework of Alenka Zupančič, as well as with Lacanian thinking on the roles played by metaphor and metonymy in the process of signification. He first became acquainted with the works of Sarah Kofman while researching the sexual politics of Freudian psychoanalysis; since then, Kofman has never been far out of mind.

Sarah Kofman (1934–1994). Professor of philosophy at Paris-Sorbonne university, author of two dozen books working with and through Nietzsche and Freud, but also a range of figures across philosophy, psychoanalysis and literature (Hoffmann, Nerval, Blanchot, Rousseau, Kant, Hegel, Comte, Kierkegaard, and so on). She was associated with the 'philosophie en effet' group also including Derrida, Lacoue-Labarthe and Nancy, while remaining fiercely independent. Much but by no means all of her work has been translated into English.

Duncan Large is Professor of European Literature and Translation at the University of East Anglia (Norwich) and Academic Director of the British Centre for Literary Translation. He has published extensively on Nietzsche and is General Editor (with Alan D. Schrift) of *The Complete Works of Friedrich Nietzsche* (Stanford University Press). He has translated Kofman's *Nietzsche and Metaphor* (1993) and a number

Paragraph 44.1 (2021): 138–140
DOI: 10.3366/para.2021.0359

www.euppublishing.com/para

of her essays. He hosted Kofman's last visit to the UK (1994) and has published several essays on aspects of her work. A recent major publication is *Untranslatability: Interdisciplinary Perspectives* (co-edited for Routledge, 2018).

John McKeane is lecturer in modern French literature at the University of Reading. He has published numerous articles on the relation between writing and thought, and is the author of *Philippe Lacoue-Labarthe: (Un)timely Meditations* (Routledge, 2015) and translator of Christophe Bident's *Maurice Blanchot: A Critical Biography* (Fordham University Press, 2018).

Ginette Michaud is Professor of French Literature at the Université de Montréal. As a member of the international committee responsible for the edition of Jacques Derrida's seminars, she has coedited *The Beast and the Sovereign* (University of Chicago Press, 2009 and 2011) and *Le parjure et le pardon* (Seuil, 2019 and 2020). She has also co-edited a collection of Derrida's writings on art, *Thinking Out of Sight* (University of Chicago Press, 2020), as well as a collection of his writings on architecture, *Les Arts de l'espace* (La Différence, 2015). She has dedicated several books to Derrida's work and co-edited the *Cahier de L'Herne Derrida* (2004), the volume *Appels de Jacques Derrida* (Hermann, 2014), *Sarah Kofman et Jacques Derrida: Croisements, écarts, différences* (Hermann, 2018) and *Sarah Kofman: philosopher autrement* (forthcoming, Hermann, 2021).

Cillian Ó Fathaigh is a Gates Cambridge Scholar at the University of Cambridge, where he recently completed his PhD on Jacques Derrida's philosophy of institutions. He has recently published a co-edited volume, *#NousSommes: Collectivity and the Digital in French Thought* (Peter Lang, 2020) and is currently preparing a substantial edited volume on Derrida's Politics of Friendship (under contract with Edinburgh University Press). He is currently working at the École Normale Supérieure de Lyon.

Elizabeth Rottenberg is Professor of Philosophy and Director of the Program in Comparative Literature at DePaul University. She is also a practising psychoanalyst in Chicago. Her most recent book is *For the Love of Psychoanalysis: The Play of Chance in Freud and Derrida* (2019).

Charlotte Thevenet holds a PhD in French Studies from University College London. Her research has focused on Derrida's double texts, and she is completing a monograph on the rhetorics of the commentary in this corpus. Her current research explores the gendered rhetorics of the abortion narrative in French and francophone women's contemporary writings.

Cosmin Toma is a British Academy Postdoctoral Fellow at the University of Oxford's Faculty of Medieval and Modern Languages. His research is chiefly concerned with modern and contemporary French literature, critical theory and aesthetics. His book, *Neutraliser l'absolu. Blanchot, Beckett et la chose littéraire* (Hermann, 2019) is an inquiry into what remains of what Nancy and Lacoue-Labarthe termed 'the literary absolute' after its encounter with modernity. He is currently finishing a second monograph — on Blanchot in the internet age — and preparing an edited volume, *Understanding Nancy, Understanding Modernism* (Bloomsbury, 2021).